Too Loud?

Too Loud?

A guide to workplace noise, its measurement and control

John Humphrey
BSc CEng MIChemE FIOSH FIRM

David Farmer
BA LLB FInst Pet FIOSH RSP

Croner Publications Ltd
Croner House
London Road
Kingston upon Thames
Surrey KT2 6SR
Tel: 081-547 3333

Copyright 1989 Kingwood
This edition first published 1989
Second edition 1990

Published by
Croner Publications Ltd,
Croner House,
London Road,
Kingston upon Thames,
Surrey KT2 6SR
Telephone 081-547 3333

British Library Cataloguing in Publication Data

Humphrey, John, *1945* –
Too Loud? – New ed. – (Croner health and
safety guides)
1. Occupational noise
I. Title II. Farmer, David, *1928* –. Too Loud?
363.7'43

ISBN 1 85524 036 X

Printed by Whitstable Litho, Whitstable,
Kent

Contents

Contents

Introduction

For a considerable time now it has been known that workplace exposure to noise beyond a certain level can lead to an irreversible deterioration in the hearing of those exposed to it.

Regulatory bodies are accordingly moving towards tougher control measures. Instruments and techniques are now available by which a worker's noise dose can be measured accurately, so it is possible to forestall the onset of noise-induced hearing loss by practicable precautionary measures. These involve consideration of design and engineering factors, and where these alone do not suffice, effective personal protective equipment is available for people to wear.

This book describes how noise affects the sense of hearing. It also examines the units of measurement for sound, and discusses the use of measurement as a feature of noise assessment and control programmes. Above all, the book reviews the range of options available to those needing to control noise.

The book also describes the existing statutory and common law position with regard to workplace noise, and the Noise at Work Regulations 1989 which bring United Kingdom legislation into line with the provisions of EC Directive 86/188/EEC.

Chapter 1

Noise-induced deafness

Sound is not only one of the valued sources of information by which we interpret and appreciate our environment; it is also an agency which can injure us. Above a certain intensity the sound pressure waves bring about a deterioration in the sensitivity of parts of the inner ear and our hearing becomes slowly, insidiously, and irreversibly damaged. Other noise-induced conditions occur such as tinnitus; loudness recruitment; and psychological effects, associated with stress, fatigue, and an inability to concentrate.

Historical background

In the early nineteenth century boilermakers, smiths and braziers were amongst the first groups of workers whose exposure to noise at work was recognised as giving rise to deafness. Appropriately enough, in the early days the condition was simply referred to as boilermakers' deafness. Later on, railway workers and weavers were added to the list of those whose jobs were noisy and where there was a strong possibility of measurable hearing loss being sustained as a result of the work they did.

By 1927 a study revealed that out of 1000 cotton weavers who had worked from between 1-64 years in cotton mills a quarter were found to have suffered some degree of deafness. The group who manifested signs of hearing impairment had all worked in the noise for more than a decade. Those with over 20 years' exposure showed a much more pronounced increase in their degree of hearing loss.

Reporting in his annual report for 1963, H M Chief Inspector of Factories told of the work of the Committee on the Problem of Noise under the chairmanship of Sir Alan Wilson. One of the Wilson Committee's recommendations was that the Ministry of Labour should disseminate existing knowledge of the hazard of noise and impress upon industry the need to do something about it. As a direct result of the Wilson Committee's recommendations, the Factory Inspectorate produced, in 1963, an advisory booklet called "Noise and the Worker". It outlined the possible harmful effects of noise and described how a noise reduction and hearing conservation programme should be conducted.

The significance of the appearance of the 1963 booklet was that it brought clearly into the public domain the fact that continuous exposure to noise was likely to cause irreversible hearing damage. Employers were put on notice that if high levels of noise were created by their activities they should do something about it. By 1972 the Factory Inspectorate had produced a Code of Practice in which it proffered guidance. The Secretary of State for Employment at the time, the Right Hon. Robert Carr, stated in his foreword to the Code, called the "Code of Practice for Reducing the Exposure of Employed Persons to Noise", that the general solution to the complex problem of noise had hitherto been hampered more by ignorance than neglect. The pioneer work of Professor Burns and Dr Robinson, published in "Hearing and Noise in Industry" (HMSO) in 1970 was acknowledged. Prior to their work we lacked the necessary scientific knowledge of the precise levels of noise and the duration of exposure to them which caused damage. The Code of Practice remedied this deficiency and provided a blueprint for action. Against this background of our acceptance that too long an exposure to too loud a noise is potentially harmful it is appropriate now to turn our attention to the organ of hearing concerned – the human ear.

The external ear

It might at first seem surprising that the ear, the organ of hearing, is damaged by sound – the stimulus it is supposed to detect. However, the human ear evolved during millions of years of relative quiet and the fact is that the current level of noise from industry and entertainment simply overloads the system.

The mechanism by which sound, in the form of atmospheric pressure waves, is converted into a signal for the brain, is highly complex. It starts with the conspicuous external part of the ear (Fig 1). This goes under a variety of names and we will use one of the more medical expressions – the pinna. The job of the pinna is to funnel sound into the next section of the ear, the auditory canal or meatus. The auditory canal is simply

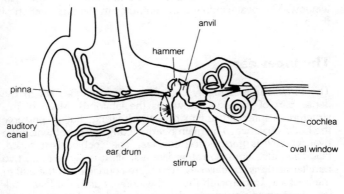

Fig 1 The ear, showing the arrangement of middle and inner ear.

a tube about 2 cm long, at the end of which is a taut membrane: the eardrum. The eardrum is set into vibration by the sound wave, and this vibration is the signal which is passed on to the next section of the ear.

The middle ear

The middle ear is a small cavity connected with the nasal cavity by the Eustachian tube. The Eustachian tube opens when we swallow so that the middle ear is kept at atmospheric pressure. A common experience is pain in the ear when this pressure equalisation mechanism is not working. This is often the result of a cold, when mucus blocks the Eustachian tube. If the external pressure then varies, as in an aeroplane on take-off or landing, there is an uncorrected pressure differential on the two sides of the eardrum which firstly causes reduced hearing sensitivity, and then pain.

Assuming, however, that all is working well, the vibrations of the eardrums are passed on to the main components of the middle ear: the ossicles. The ossicles are three minute, connected bones: the malleus, incus and stapes, commonly known as the hammer, anvil and stirrup. These make up a small system of levers and are designed to amplify the vibrations on the eardrum. The amplified signal is transferred by the stirrup to another diaphragm, smaller than the eardrum: the oval window. The oval window is the entrance to the final section of the ear.

The inner ear

The inner ear is a highly complex series of tubes set in the dense part of the skull known as the labyrinth. Much of this structure is intended not to measure hearing, but to preserve the body's balance. The main hearing component, of which the oval window is part, is the cochlea. The cochlea is a coiled, fluid-filled tube, looking rather like a snail. It is divided into two parallel sections, or galleries, which are connected at the end of the cochlea. Underneath the oval window, but in the lower gallery, is another diaphragm, the round window. The round window is sufficiently flexible to allow the fluid in the cochlea to transmit the vibrations from the oval window.

It is the inner walls of the cochlea that contain the real mechanism of hearing. The cochlea is lined with about 20,000 fibres, often known as hair cells (Fig 2). These fibres are connected to the nerve endings of the auditory nerve, which leads to the brain. Thus, the hair cells, picking up the vibration from the fluid in the cochlea, generate signals in the nerve which will be interpreted by the brain as the experience of sound or, if the experience is unpleasant, noise.

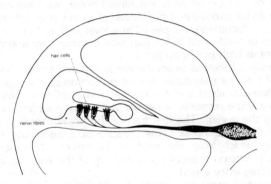

Fig 2 Diagram showing a cross-section of the cochlea.

The hair cells are, of course, doing more than merely detecting whether sound is present or not. They respond, with remarkable sensitivity, to variations in the loudness and frequency of sound. This enables complex signals like speech and music to be analysed for their information content, or their aesthetic value. However, the exact mechanism by which the ear assesses differences in the quality of sound, is not clear. A number of theories exist, ranging from the suggestion that different hair cells respond to different sound frequencies, to a theory based on the creation of holographic interference patterns within the inner ear. Whatever the mechanism, the hair cells are the key to hearing and to deafness caused by noise. They are the most sensitive component in a complex structure and, when the system is overloaded, are the first to break down.

13

Overloading

In the last two centuries or so, the human ear has been subject to bombardment with noise, quite unlike the environment in which it evolved. This is primarily because the machinery which has dominated our lives since the industrial revolution is not completely efficient. Not all of the energy in an engine goes to drive the shaft, nor all of the energy in a power press to stamping the component. Instead, energy is lost to the environment in the form of heat and noise. In addition to, and perhaps because of, our exposure to machinery noise, we have acquired the taste for exposure to high levels of sound as entertainment. Music in discotheques is played at a level well up to high industrial noise levels, and hi-fi equipment is commonly sold on the basis of its high power output level.

So what happens when the ear is exposed to high levels of noise? Firstly it introduces its own protection mechanisms. It is not always realised that the ear has some ability to protect itself, since the response is neither visible nor voluntary (as, say, closing the eyelid). The first part of the protection response is called the aural reflex. This consists of a tightening of the muscles which keep the eardrum in tension. The increased eardrum tension reduces the sensitivity of the ear, particularly to low frequency sound.

A second protective mechanism is introduced if the ear is subject to extremely loud noise. It consists of a change in the way the ossicles, the three bones in the middle ear, vibrate. Instead of directly transmitting vibration from the eardrum to the oval window, the ossicles start to rock from side to side. This greatly reduces the efficiency of the system and there is a substantial reduction in loudness.

Damage

Unfortunately, the ear's own protection mechanisms are not adequate to cope with the excesses of today's noisy environment. They fail firstly because the aural reflex takes a few milliseconds to come into operation. This means that noise resulting from impacts (such as a hammer hitting metal) which have a very short time duration, will penetrate the unprotected ear. Secondly, the in-built protection is inadequate to cope with high, sustained noise levels, day after day, week after week. That the ear is ill-equipped to handle impact noise and sustained high level noise is not surprising since these are circumstances which do not occur in nature. Rather than wait for a few million years of evolution, we are thus obliged to introduce artificial measures to protect us against this recent exposure.

The problem, as already suggested, lies with the hair cells in the cochlea. When subject to excessive vibration they become physically damaged. As a result, the strength of signal to the auditory nerve is reduced, and the victim suffers progressive deafness.

If the exposure to noise is reasonably short, and the level not too great, the resulting deafness is temporary. This is described as a temporary threshold shift, which means that the lowest level of noise which can just be heard is increased for a period of time. The higher the noise level and the longer the exposure, the greater is the threshold shift, and the longer the time for hearing to return to normal. Substantial exposure to high industrial noise can result in a temporary threshold shift which has not recovered by the time the sufferer returns to work the next day. The next period of noise exposure thus reinforces the level and duration of the deafness.

Temporary threshold shift is likely to be accompanied by the unpleasant experience of tinnitus. This is a constant buzzing or ringing in the ears, felt by many deafness victims to be a worse affliction than the loss of hearing.

Deafness

As stated, the threshold shift resulting from damage to the hair cells is temporary, provided the noise exposure is not too great, and there is a sufficient period in a quiet environment for the ear to recover. A common analogy to explain this is the damage to a field of wheat after strong wind. The wheat is compared to the hair cells and it is suggested that provided the wind is moderate, the wheat will recover in the calm weather which follows.

Farming colleagues tell me this is a poor comparison and that flattened wheat never actually recovers! Be that as it may, it does seem that the flattened hair cells can spring back into action with the result that hearing returns to normal.

However, this sequence of damage and recovery cannot go on indefinitely. If noise exposure is repeated day after day, the recovery is not complete and a degree of permanent deafness sets in. This is because the repeated stressing of the hair cells weakens them to the point where they fracture. The consequent loss of hearing sensitivity is then irreparable since the hair cell has no capacity for regeneration.

A major problem with deafness arising in this way, is that its onset is slow and insidious. Victims are very unlikely to realise that they are going deaf because on each occasion of noise exposure they lose so few of their 20,000 hair cells that they cannot perceive the difference in hearing sensitivity. In addition they may be experiencing a cycle of temporary threshold shift, in which the hearing appears to have recovered each morning, which masks the relentless progression towards deafness from which they are not recovering.

Victims will, at first, make adjustments for their deafness. They will increase the volume of the television. They will suspect that members of the family are beginning to mumble. They will compensate by unknowingly lip-reading. Everything will be heard as if through cotton wool, but so gradual is the change that they do not recognise it as a handicap until it is too late.

An important characteristic of noise-induced deafness is that the loss of hearing is not the same at all frequencies. We will look at the unit of frequency measurement, the Hertz, in the next chapter. It is sufficient to say here that the main loss of sensitivity is to sounds around 4000 Hertz. Unfortunately, this is a very important frequency for speech communication – it means that consonant sounds, such as "t" and "m" will not be heard, resulting in the feeling that sounds are muffled. In other words noise induced deafness, especially in its early stages, is a distortion of hearing rather than a uniform reduction of sensitivity to all sounds. A most serious consequence of this is that noise-induced deafness cannot be corrected by using a hearing aid. The hearing aid will merely amplify the distorted signal and will not restore the vital information content in the 4000 Hertz area which has been lost for ever.

Individual susceptibility

Like many chronic illnesses caused by workplace exposures, noise-induced deafness affects some individuals more severely than others. Thus, after exposure to the same level of noise for the same length of time, some individuals might become substantially deaf, whilst others might escape largely unscathed. As we will see later, this presents a major problem in devising noise legislation – should it protect most people, or everyone? Unfortunately, there is no way of identifying the particularly susceptible individuals until they actually start to go deaf.

The graph (Fig 3) shows an estimate of the percentage of a typical industrial population which will suffer hearing loss after exposure to noise. Again, units are defined in the next chapter.

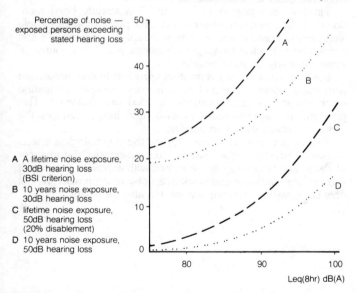

A A lifetime noise exposure, 30dB hearing loss (BSI criterion)
B 10 years noise exposure, 30dB hearing loss
C lifetime noise exposure, 50dB hearing loss (20% disablement)
D 10 years noise exposure, 50dB hearing loss

Fig 3 Hearing loss in a typical industrial population at 65 years of age (HSE estimate). Based on graph in HSC Consultative Document "Protection of Hearing at Work".

Taking some figures from the graph it will be seen that, at age

65, about 40% of those exposed to a lifetime noise exposure of 90 dB(A) will experience more than 30 dB hearing loss whilst about 10% will suffer a more serious hearing loss in excess of 50 dB.

Other effects

This book is concerned primarily with the prevention of noise-induced deafness. This is a permanent, disabling affliction which isolates people from the world and excludes them from a wide range of social activity. However, it is worth noting that noise has other undesirable effects.

Tinnitus, or "ringing in the ear" has already been mentioned. It is a permanent condition in a proportion of people with noise-induced deafness. It is incessant and inescapable and cannot be corrected by surgery. Tinnitus is a major source of stress for many deafness victims.

Loudness recruitment is another common feature associated with noise induced hearing loss. It is the experience of hearing some sounds as disproportionately loud and distorted. This phenomenon is unpleasant in itself, and further reduces the ability to understand communication.

Finally, but difficult to quantify, are the psychological effects of noise. Stress, fatigue, inability to concentrate, disturbances of sleep, are all commonly associated with exposure to noise. It is therefore inevitable that work in a noisy environment will not only be hazardous and unpleasant, but also inefficient.

Chapter 2

Measurement

The principal purpose of measuring sound at work is to identify areas in which the level is injurious to those exposed to it. To arrive at this point we must know about both loudness and frequency, and develop units of measurement which can be utilised to indicate when a worker's noise dose approaches the danger level. Sophisticated instruments exist to do this, and measuring techniques also exist to assess an individual's degree of hearing sensitivity (audiometry).

Difficulties

Measuring noise presents a difficulty. It is that noise is not a measurable physical property, like heat or light, but is a subjective experience created within the brain. The dictionary definition of noise is "unwanted sound" and the "unwanted" qualification will vary from time to time and from person to person.

In practice however, sound and noise are invariably associated with a measurable physical phenomenon. That is a wave of oscillating pressure travelling through the air. This wave emanates from a vibrating object. As the object vibrates outwards, it slightly compresses the air next to it. However, air is an elastic or "springy" medium and instead of staying compressed, the air bounces back into a state of slightly reduced pressure. Whilst this is happening, the next "layer" of air is also being affected. When layer one expands, layer two will be compressed and vice versa. And so it goes on with the pressure variations being passed through the air until they fade out through dissipation and loss of energy. If we plot a graph of the pressure variations in the air, we get a wavy line showing the pressure rising and falling either side of normal atmospheric pressure (Fig 4).

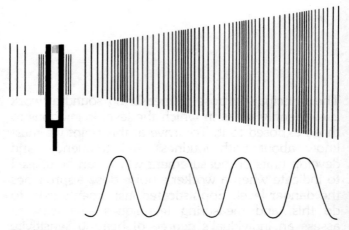

Fig 4 Diagrammatic representation of sound pressure waves.

On the face of it, measurement of sound or noise should now be straightforward, since our pressure wave can be fully defined with only two measurements.

These are the height or amplitude of the wave, which will indicate how loud the sound is and the distance apart of the waves, which will give the sound's frequency. In practice, there are a number of complications.

Loudness

Loudness is a function of the magnitude of pressure variations in the atmosphere as the sound wave passes through. The greater the variation, the more will the sound deflect the ear-drum, and the greater will be the signal via the auditory nerve to the brain. We can therefore measure loudness in units of pressure. The problem with doing this is that the human ear is sensitive across a remarkably wide range of pressure variation. If we were measuring pressure in Newtons per square metre, the range of human hearing would be from around 0.00002 to 20,000. In other words, we would have to use a scale with a range of about a billion units. In practice, we are simply not accustomed to coping with scales of this size, and the scale is therefore compressed by taking the logarithm to the base 10 of our unwieldy unit. The logarithm is not in fact taken directly from the pressure of the noise, but from its intensity, or amount of energy falling on a fixed area. In addition, in order to avoid awkward units, the intensity is divided by a fixed reference intensity. Since the intensity is proportional to the square of the pressure, we can now write our unit of loudness as:

$$\log_{10} \frac{p^2}{pr^2}$$

where p is the sound pressure level, and pr is the reference pressure.

The reference pressure is set at the assumed threshold of hearing (the lowest pressure to which the ear will respond) of 0.00002 Newtons/m^2.

The unit defined above is called the Bel. It is named after Alexander Graham Bell, the American inventor. Bell is most noted for the invention of the telephone but, appropriately, he also devoted a good deal of his life to the teaching of the deaf. The Bel has in fact compressed the noise scale rather too much and gives an everyday range from 0 to about 15. The scale is therefore expanded by 10 to give the common unit of noise intensity, the decibel, with a range from 0 at the hearing threshold to about 150 – a level loud enough to cause pain. So, the full formula for the decibel is now:

$$10\log_{10} \frac{P^2}{pr^2}$$

We have not yet finished with the decibel but, before discussing it further, we must consider the other characteristic of sound, its frequency.

Frequency

The frequency of sound or noise is simply the rate at which the pressure fluctuation in the atmosphere varies. Rapid variations represent a high frequency sound and the effect, in terms of subjective experience, is of a high pitched note. Slow variations produce low frequency sounds.

Measurement units are straightforward: the number of pressure oscillations which occur in one second are counted and expressed as cycles per second.

To complicate matters slightly, the cycle per second is now generally referred to as the Hertz, after the German scientist Heinrich Hertz who studied wave motion in electro-magnetic radiation. The abbreviation for Hertz is Hz.

Now comes the real problem – the human ear does not hear all frequencies of sound equally well. Sounds with a lower frequency than about 20Hz, and a higher frequency than about 20,000Hz, we do not hear at all. Within the sounds that we do hear, the "audible range", the sensitivity of the ear varies considerably. Maximum sensitivity is at about 3000Hz, with sensitivity falling off above and below this point.

The fact that the ear has a different sensitivity at different frequencies has an important implication. It is that the decibel cannot be used as a true measure of loudness. The reason is that two sounds could have equal decibel levels (ie they would be creating the same pressure fluctuation in the atmosphere), but if one sound had a frequency at which the ear is highly sensitive, say 3000Hz, and the other sound had a frequency at which the ear has poor sensitivity, say 500Hz, they would sound very different. Because the ear is so much better at detecting the 3000Hz sound, it would judge it to be louder than the 500Hz sound. In fact, even though the mathematical decibel levels are exactly the same, the 3000Hz sound would be judged to be about 20 decibels louder.

The A-weighted decibel

Loudness, as perceived by the human ear and brain, is a function of both the intensity and the frequency of the sound

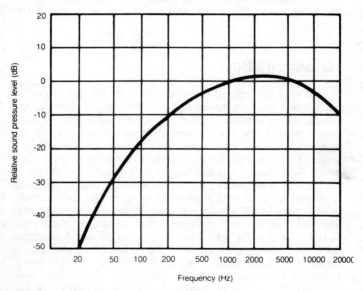

Fig 5 The A-weighting curve for sound level meters

pressure wave and this means that any unit of true loudness must take both factors into account. This is achieved by taking the decibel level, as already defined, and correcting it according to the frequency of the sound. Thus, sounds at frequencies which the ear does not hear well have large correction factors, or "weighting" factors, applied so that the resulting decibel level more closely resembles the level that the ear actually hears.

A number of attempts have been made to define exactly what weighting factors should be applied to each frequency. A complication is that the factors themselves vary according to the intensity of the sound. However, for the vast majority of applications, the weighting factors are universally agreed and are usually presented as a curve – the "A"-weighting curve (Fig 5). The shape of this curve is also, of course, a plot of the variation in sensitivity of the ear with frequency. A decibel level to which the appropriate A-weighting has been applied is known as an "A-weighted decibel", abbreviated to dB(A). This unit has wide acceptance as a realistic measure of loudness. *It is the basis for noise standards and legislation throughout the world.*

Measuring dB(A)

In reviewing the units of sound and noise so far, reference has been made to "the frequency" of a sound. In practice, the sounds we experience in everyday life are an incredibly complex mixture made up of many different frequencies. For all that, however, it is always possible to unravel the sound into a series of simple pressure sine waves superimposed upon each other. Nevertheless, the business of sorting out a sound into its component frequencies, and then applying the appropriate A-weighting, involves considerable measurement and calculation. Fortunately, the increased interest in noise has coincided with the development of sophisticated integrated electronics. This means that the job of producing a combined A-weighted decibel from a complex noise can be undertaken instantly by a compact portable sound level meter. We expose the microphone of the meter to the noise, and read off the dB(A) level from a dial or a digital display. See Fig 6 – Diagram of elements of a sound level meter.

Estimating dB(A) level

Having shown the origin of this complex unit, the dB(A), it is interesting to look at the actual levels of some common sounds. At the bottom of the range, it is theoretically possible to hear a level of 0dB(A). This is because the sound pressure level is then at the defined threshold of hearing - the reference pressure in the equation of the decibel. In practice, though, the quietest sounds that most of us can hear are likely to be more than 20dB(A). This would be the level of a quiet breeze in the countryside with no contribution from traffic.

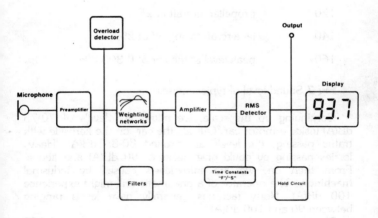

Fig 6 Elements of a sound level meter

Such an experience is now rare, and the lowest level we are likely to find in our houses, with no television on and no traffic noise, is about 35 dB(A). Once we add noise from conversation, television, etc, the level rises to perhaps 65 dB(A).

25

dB(A)	
25	still day in the country
35	quiet bedroom
45	quiet office
65	busy office
75	inside motor car
85	typical factory production line
95	noisy factory area
105	extremely noisy heavy engineering factory
120	propeller aircraft at 25m
140	jet aircraft taking off at 25m
160	peak level at the ear of 0.303 rifle

Fig 7 Sound level of typical noises

Continuing up the scale, we might find levels of 70-75 dB(A) inside a motor car. Outside the car, on the kerbside with traffic passing, the levels are around 80-85 dB(A). Heavy lorries passing by could give peaks of 90 dB(A) and above. From then on, we are into levels caused by industrial machinery. The operator of a pneumatic drill might experience 100 dB(A). Noisy factories generally have levels ranging between 90 and 100 dB(A).

The commonest source of noise levels in excess of 100 dB(A) is the aeroplane. Close proximity (25 metres) to a propellor aeroplane on take-off, gives a level typically around 120 dB(A). A jet aeroplane is closer to 140 dB(A). Levels beyond this are certainly not unknown, but are more likely to be experienced as peak rather than sustained levels. For example, a rifle shot might give a peak of 160 dB(A) at the ear of the user.

Figure 7 shows some typical noise levels across the scale of normal human experience.

Noise dose

Complicated though the dB(A) is, we now have to add yet another complication.

This is because we are concerned with the way noise varies with time. Exposure to noise during say, a working day, will not be to a steady, fixed dB(A) level, but to levels which are rising and falling as we move around, and use different machinery. Our real requirement is therefore not to know the dB(A) level at any particular time, but to know the dose of noise which has been received during the day.

The calculation of noise dose can be difficult. This is because the dB(A) level may be continually rising and falling, and because the logarithmic nature of the dB(A) adds a further complication in any calculation. However, the unit that emerges from the exercise is the equivalent continuous sound level, abbreviated to L_{EP}.

The L_{EP} is the steady level of noise which would have given the same noise dose over the measuring period, as the actual varying levels. It is also necessary to specify the period of measurement, and this is usually taken as 8 hours, to relate to a normal working day. The unit is then written $L_{EP,d}$.

As with measuring the dB(A), modern electronics spares us much of the potential complication. A noise meter with an L_{EP} facility continually monitors the noise level and then gives an L_{EP} reading for whatever time it has been in use. It should be noted that an $L_{EP,d}$ does not necessarily require 8 hours of measurement. It is simply that the noise which has been measured is averaged and spread out as though it had lasted 8 hours.

Working with the units

We have now derived some remarkably complicated units. As the book proceeds they will become more familiar, but it is worth pointing out that since the dB(A) is a logarithmic unit, it cannot be incorporated directly into arithmetic calculations. For example, if we have a machine producing a noise level of 90 dB(A), and place a similar machine beside it, the resulting level is not 180 dB(A). This is because doubling a number causes its

27

logarithm to increase by 0.3. Doubling sound intensity therefore results in a rise of 0.3 Bels or 3 decibels. The two 90 dB(A) machines therefore will only produce a new noise level of 93 dB(A).

The 3 dB(A) doubling criterion can be useful in assessing L_{EP} or noise dose. For example, one way of experiencing an L_{EP} (8hr) of 90 dB(A) (an important standard in the United Kingdom, as we will see in the next chapter), is to be exposed to a level of 90 dB(A) for 8 hours. However, we could receive the same noise dose through exposure to twice the noise level for half the time. In other words to 93 dB(A) for four hours. This enables us to build up a table of noise levels and exposure times, all of which meet a given standard. For example:

90 dB(A) $L_{EP,d}$
90 dB(A) for 8 hours
93 dB(A) for 4 hours
96 dB(A) for 2 hours
99 dB(A) for 1 hour
102 dB(A) for 30 minutes
105 dB(A) for 15 minutes

Impact noise

We have now developed the concept of the noise dose – in other words the amount of energy received by the ear over a period of time. This is important in the development of noise standards and legislation, since it is the dose rather than the simple noise level, which does the damage. However, there is one circumstance in which the total dose is ignored, and the level is the important measurement. This is when the noise is of extremely short duration – but is extremely loud. In other words, an impact noise. Examples would be explosions and metal surfaces impacting together.

Whilst the total energy entering the ear from an impact noise may be small because of the short duration there is still potential for harm. This is partly because the high level can enter the ear before natural protection mechanisms have come into action. Legislation, therefore, specifies a "peak action level" at which action must be taken – even if the personal noise dose does not exceed the action limits. The peak action level is usually expressed as a sound pressure level with the pressure units of pascals. The current peak action level is 200 pascals – actually equivalent to a noise level of about 140 decibels.

Audiometry

In this chapter we have so far been concerned with measurement of the characteristics of the sound or noise emanating from a source. Before concluding the review of measurement we should consider another measurable factor – the hearing sensitivity of an individual.

The measurement of hearing sensitivity or acuity is called audiometry and consists of playing pure tone sounds (ie sound of a single frequency) through headphones worn by the subject. Each ear is tested in turn and the lowest level at which the sound can be heard is recorded. The test is repeated at a number of pure tones, usually 125, 250, 500, 1000, 1500, 2000, 3000, 4000, 6000 and 8000Hz, and the graph of sensitivity at each of these frequencies is known as an audiogram. The audiogram is generally presented as the hearing loss, in decibels, at each frequency as compared with normal hearing.

As with the measurement of noise, audiometry is greatly simplified by modern electronics and instrumentation. Once set up, many audiometers will automatically plot an audiogram, the subject having merely to press a button when he or she can hear the sounds. However, audiometric testing nevertheless requires trained supervision and proper surroundings. It is also essential to ensure that the person being tested has had an appropriate period of time in a quiet environment to ensure that he or she is not suffering from any temporary threshold shift.

One of the reasons for the importance of audiometry in hearing conservation programmes – and indeed in legal proceedings – is that the audiogram can often differentiate between deafness caused by noise, and deafness resulting from other causes. This is because, as was noted in Chapter 1, noise induced deafness starts with a loss of sensitivity to sounds with a frequency around 4000 Hertz. Thus the victim's audiogram shows a characteristic "dip" at this frequency. To succeed in a claim for noise induced deafness, the plantiff would be expected to show audiometry results with this particular feature.

Audiometry as a feature of a company's noise control programme is sometimes criticised as "shutting the stable door after the horse has bolted". In other words, it measures deafness after the damage is done, rather than contributing to the *prevention* of deafness. This may be rather unfair, since the deafness measured by audiometry may be at a sufficiently early stage to enable precautionary measures to prevent further deterioration. However, the criticism does raise an important point which is often overlooked – what *is* one going to do with the results? It would clearly be irresponsible to be acquiring the knowledge that certain employees were going deaf, without having a plan of action to respond to such results. The plan probably needs to include the retraining of such individuals in the use of protectors, the remeasuring of their hearing at regular intervals and, possibly, their relocation to less noisy areas.

One motivation for introducing audiometry programmes is to establish a baseline of hearing acuity for new employees. This is essentially to ensure that any subsequent claims for deafness are known to relate genuinely to hearing deterioration during the current period of employment – and not, perhaps, with some previous employer.

Audiometry may be able to differentiate between deafness caused by noise and that resulting from other causes. However, it is unlikely to be able to identify the source of the noise which caused the deafness. This raises the possibility that someone presenting a case for work-induced deafness is actually suffering from leisure-induced deafness. Many leisure pursuits are increasingly noisy – a particular concern is with high volume music which may be played for long periods of time through the headphones of portable cassette players. Whilst the audiogram may not resolve this question, a deafness claim will probably not succeed unless it can be shown that the amount of deafness revealed by audiometry relates to the claimed exposure to noise in the workplace.

When new noise legislation was being framed, there was a strong expectation that audiometry would become a legal requirement in certain circumstances. This was because the United Kingdom had to respond to an EC directive requiring that audiometry was made available to some groups of employees. In practice, no mandatory provision of audiometry was introduced on the grounds that hearing testing is already available through the NHS. However, the Health and Safety Executive has undertaken to keep the whole subject of audiometry under review, and we may yet see new legal requirements.

Chapter 3

The law

After a period of statutory consultation United Kingdom legislation was brought into conformity with the European directive on the protection of workers from the adverse effects of noise on 1.1.90. Both the content and implications of the statutory requirements imposed on employers to control noise, and the position of those suffering noise induced hearing loss and seeking redress from those they allege to be responsible, are reviewed.

In the second edition of the book the text of this chapter was based upon the Health and Safety Commission's proposals for new regulations contained in the consultative document "Prevention of damage to hearing from noise at work – Draft proposals for Regulations and Guidance" HMSO, November 1987. The consultative document had in its turn been drafted in conformity with the terms of the EC Directive on "The protection of workers from the risks related to exposure to noise at work" 86/188/EEC. This directive was adopted on 12.5.86, and set to take effect in all but two Member States by 1.1.90. (In the cases of Greece and Portugal, because of the date of their joining the Community, the date for implementation was set at 1.1.91.)

There will be a re-examination of the directive before 1.1.94 in the light of progress made in scientific knowledge and technology. The re-examination will also take into account experience gained by that time by Member States in the implementation of the directive in its present form.

In the event, the assumption that the regulations would not differ significantly from the 1987 consultative document proposals turned out to be true. Now, however, the resulting Noise at Work Regulations 1989 have come into operation and their contents are studied in detail later on in the chapter.

Legislative challenge

In Chapter 1 it was seen that the hazard of noise must be expressed in terms of probabilities. In other words, at any given noise level a certain percentage of the exposed population is at risk. Hazards of this sort present a major challenge for legislators because they must decide how many people the law should protect. The size of the problem in Great Britain has been estimated and is shown in the table shown in Fig 8. The estimate is based on a survey of the exposure of production workers made in 1976 in a random sample of approaching five hundred manufacturing establishments. The figures shown have been suitably adjusted to take into account the changes between 1976 and 1986 in the total numbers employed in the industries concerned. Although information about the position in other industries is not so reliable the Health and Safety

Executive has estimated that the proportion is about the same in the mining industry. It is further estimated that in construction, agriculture, forestry, quarrying, shipping, transport, railway-work, and entertainment there are some areas with noise levels above the two relevant action levels referred to in the directive. The estimates are that about 1.7 million workers may be exposed above 85 dB(A) and between half and three quarters of a million above 90 dB(A).

At first the answer might seem obvious: the law should protect everyone. However, if this was achieved by setting a statutory maximum noise level at which no one would be affected, that level would be so low as to be virtually unattainable by most industries. Framing legislation therefore involves a compromise between reducing the risk and setting a realistic standard.

Fig 8 Estimated number of persons exposed to noise in manufacturing industry

noise exposure $L_{EP,d}$	85-90 dB(A)	90-95 dB(A)	95-100 dB(A)	100-110 dB(A)	over 110 dB(A)
number of persons (000s)	710	275	115	34.5	2.5
% of all employees in manufacturing industry	13.8	5.4	2.2	0.7	less than 0.1

Note: The estimate is based on a survey of the exposure of production workers made in 1976, in a random sample of 488 manufacturing establishments. The figures have been adjusted to reflect the change between 1976 and 1986 in the total number employed in these industries (December 1986 total = 5,136,000).

Statute law

It might seem surprising that, although the hazard of noise had been recognised since the 1960s, there was very little statute law in the United Kingdom which dealt directly with the subject. There were five exceptions:

(a) The Woodworking Machines Regulations 1974, required that noise should be reduced to the greatest extent which was reasonably practicable, and that ear protectors should be provided and used when people were likely to be exposed at or above 90dB(A) Leq (8hr). Regulation 44 of the Woodworking Machines Regulations 1974 was revoked by Regulation 15 of the Noise at Work Regulations 1989 on 1.1.90.

(b) The Agriculture (Tractor Cabs) Regulations 1974 set a maximum level of 90dB(A) in the criteria for the approval of safety cabs.

(c) The Offshore Installations (Construction and Survey) Regulations 1974, and the Offshore Installations (Operational Safety, Health and Welfare) Regulations 1976, require the insulation of equipment capable of causing injurious noise, and provision of suitable protective equipment, including ear protection, for those at risk.

There were also regulations covering merchant shipping which deal with the noise hazard.

Beyond these exceptions, the subject of noise did not appear specifically in any statute law concerned directly with the workplace.

Under the Control of Pollution Act 1974, however, a local authority is enabled to take summary proceedings in respect of a noise which is established as a nuisance. Workplace noise is one of the commoner sources of noise nuisance complaints. Employers seeking to mitigate noise inside their premises for the benefit of employees could possibly, by such action, create a noise nuisance for neighbours, eg by moving a noisy machine such as a compressor to an outside location. Having said that there are few specific statutory references to noise, this does not mean that there had not been a general statutory requirement to reduce noise levels overall, and reduce the exposure of employees to noise levels likely to be harmful to their health.

Fig 9 Summary of notices issued by HSE inspectors in respect of noise
(*all improvement notices unless specified otherwise in footnotes*)

Year	Total Issued	NOTICES ISSUED IN RESPECT OF			
		HSW Act (Section 2)	HSW Act (Section 3)	Woodworking Machines Regs. 1974 (Reg. 44)	Agricultural Tractor Cabs Regs. 1974
1976	25	6	0	19	–
1977	22	4	1	17	–
1978	65	7	0	58	–
1979	74	4	0	70	–
1980	68	20	0	48	–
1981	44	21	1	22	–
1982	58	26	0	32	–
1983	67	36[1]	0	31	–
1984	134	74[2]	0	60	–
1985	133	51	1	81	–
1986[3]	22	8[4]	0	14	–
1986/87[5]	71	43[4]	3[6]	25	–
1987/88	72	29	–	33	10
1988/89 (provisional)	55[7]	28	–	20	6
TOTALS	910[7]	357	6	530	16

Notes
(1) *Includes three Immediate Prohibition Notices*
(2) *Includes three Immediate and one Deferred Prohibition Notices*
(3) *January to March only*
(4) *Includes two Immediate and one Deferred Prohibition Notices*
(5) *Planning year March 1986 to April 1987*
(6) *Includes one Deferred Prohibition Notice*
(7) *Includes one notice under Construction Workplaces Regulations*

S. 2 of the Health and Safety at Work, etc Act 1974 reads "It shall be the duty of every employer to ensure, so far as is reasonably practicable, the health, safety and welfare at work of all his employees". There is no doubt whatsoever that the hazard of noise had to be dealt with as part of this broad based duty placed upon the shoulders of employers by the 1974 Act. The Director General of the Health and Safety Executive is on record as saying in 1984 that the 1972 "Code of Practice for Reducing the Exposure of Employed Persons to Noise" would be used by inspectors in the enforcement of employers' duties under the 1974 Act. The number of notices issued by inspectors since 1984 had increased significantly in line with the HSE Director General's declaration on policy. The Code, which was *not* an Approved Code of Practice made under the provisions of s. 16 of the Health and Safety At Work, etc Act 1974, was nevertheless one which indicated what criteria were being used by the HSE to indicate what they believed to be reasonably practicable standards to achieve. The 1972 Code set a limit of 90dB(A) Leq (8hr) above which employees should not be exposed. At this juncture, it is appropriate to consider what happened after the combination of the 1972 Code of Practice and the 1974 Act first established the guidelines which it was expected industry would follow to deal with the hazards to employees from noise.

Proposals for new legislation

In 1981 the Health and Safety Commission published a document containing its proposals for new noise regulations. These were extensive and received generally encouraging comment from those concerned. In the midst of the consideration of the comments made on the 1981 Consultative Document there was a proposal from the European Commission (CEC) for a European Community directive requiring Member States to harmonise their basic legislation on the protection of their workforces from noise at the workplace. In view of this proposal, published in 1982, it was clearly thought to be inappropriate that the United Kingdom should continue developing its own proposals for noise control when the European Community was also undertaking a similar task. The plans for a Community directive proved controversial mainly because of the proposal to set a single action level/limit of 85dB(A). After discussion by the European Parliament and the Council of Ministers, the proposal for the directive was amended to include two action levels – 85dB(A) and 90dB(A). The agreed Directive (86/188/EEC) was finally adopted in May 1986 and had to be implemented in most Member States (including the United Kingdom) by 1.1.90. This target was achieved. The Noise at Work Regulations 1989 were made on 2.10.89 and were laid before Parliament on 5.10.89. They came into effect on 1.1.90.

The Health and Safety Commission of the United Kingdom had published a further set of proposals for legislative changes in a Consultative Document: "Prevention of damage to hearing from noise at work – Draft proposals for Regulations and Guidance" HMSO. The period for making comments on these proposals, made in the light of the contents of the directive, ended on 30.6.88, and the final stages in the preparation of the United Kingdom's regulations proceeded. The intimation was given that the Government would make regulations ahead of the deadline of 1.1.90 to allow industry time to assimilate what needed to be done.

The Noise at Work Regulations 1989, SI 1989 No. 1790

After the prolonged consultations referred to, the regulations controlling noise as a workplace hazard are now fully in operation and apply across industry and commerce with very few exceptions.

Exceptions and applications

The duties imposed by the regulations do not extend to the master or crew of a sea-going ship nor to the employer of such persons in relation to the activities of the crews of the ships under their master's direction. Nor do the duties extend to the crew of aircraft or hovercraft moving under their own power, nor to any others on board such craft working in connection with their operation (Noise at Work Regulations 1989 (NAW), Regulation 3).

It is appropriate to bear in mind also that although the regulations apply principally for the purpose of protecting employees whose hearing may be put at risk by injurious levels of noise at work, there is a requirement for employers, so far as is reasonably practicable, to be under the same duty in relation to any other persons at work who may be affected by the noise created by that work (NAW, Regulation 2).

Contractors working side by side on a construction site or contractors working in close proximity to one another on a ship whilst it is being built, repaired or re-fitted are examples of activities where the control of noise will entail close liaison between all concerned to achieve a satisfactory standard of compliance.

If workplace noise creates risks to persons other than workers however, then the duty to control the noise is contained in s. 3 of the Health and Safety at Work, etc Act 1974 and *not* in the Noise at Work Regulations 1989. Some college students could fall into this category if their studies involve noisy plant or machinery (eg turbines, textile machines or internal combustion engines).

The self-employed are brought within the scope of the regulations by making references to employers' and employees' duties respectively applying also to the self-employed. Depending upon the situation, a self-employed person can assume the role either of employer or employee or both, as appropriate.

The duties under the Noise at Work Regulations 1989 (hereafter abbreviated to NAW) place responsibilities for compliance on employers, the self-employed, employees and the manufacturers of articles for use at work. The main requirements are as follows.

Reduction of risk of hearing damage

Apart from any specific steps referred to later, every employer is under a statutory duty to reduce the risk of damage to the hearing of his or her employees from exposure to noise *to the lowest level reasonably practicable* (Regulation 6).

It has to be appreciated that this is an important principle which reflects the general duty on all employers under s. 2 of the Health and Safety at Work, etc Act 1974.

It also has to be appreciated that because the duty is qualified by the "reasonably practicable" caveat, s. 40 of the Health and Safety at Work, etc Act 1974 requires the employer to be in a position to prove that it was not reasonably practicable to do more than was in fact done to satisfy the duty. It should be noted, however, that where a prosecution is taken under normal circumstances, it is the prosecutor who has to prove beyond reasonable doubt that what is alleged is actually the case. Where the onus of proof lies with the accused, as where s. 40 applies, the tribunal only has to be satisfied on the balance of probabilities that what the employer has done meets the "reasonably practicable" criterion.

To determine what is reasonably practicable the employer may weigh the potential risk created by the noise exposure against the cost (in money, time and trouble) involved in reducing it. Measures must be taken unless their cost is disproportionately high in relation to the benefit they yield.

Assessment of the potential risk should take account of modern information about the relationship between noise exposure and the damage to hearing. Guidance is available from official sources (HSC and HSE) and from some of the guidance in British Standard 5330: 1976 "Method of test for estimating the risk of hearing handicap due to noise exposure".

As will be seen later, the regulations operate by reference to what have been described as "action levels" which are key terms defined in NAW (Regulation 2).

There are three "action levels". The "first action level" is when an employee receives a daily personal noise exposure of 85dB(A); the "second action level" when a daily personal noise exposure of 90dB(A) is received, and the "peak action level" when a peak sound pressure wave of 200 pascals is encountered. What this means in practice is not important at this stage except to realise that it is accepted that some element of damage may occur to hearing at levels below the action levels just cited.

In other words, there is a measurable risk of hearing damage between 85dB(A) and 90dB(A), and also a small risk of adverse effects below 85dB(A). It can be seen that quite apart from the specific things which the employer is called upon to do by the regulations themselves at the particular action levels, the prudent employer will also be well advised to consider whether it is reasonably practicable to do more to control noise levels overall.

The standards in NAW are statutorily endorsed minimum standards, but there is every good reason to aim at better standards of protection in the longer term in view of Article 10 of the EC directive of May 1986 which intimates that the Council of the european Communities will re-examine the directive before 1.1.94.

The re-examination will take into account, in particular, progress made in scientific knowledge and technology as well as experience gained in the application of the directive with a view to reducing the risks arising from exposure to noise. It is highly unlikely that standards will be relaxed and every possibility that they will be made more stringent.

Reduction of noise exposure

Apart from the fundamental duty described above, to reduce the risk of damage to hearing, it has already been intimated that the regulations contain much more in the way of specific duties.

When *any* employee is *likely to be exposed* to 90dB(A) or above, or to 200 pascals or above, the employer must reduce that exposure "so far as is reasonably practicable" other than by the provision of personal ear protectors (Regulation 7).

To limit exposure every employer will need to adopt an effective programme, the elements in which, as advised in guidance from the Health and Safety Executive, include:

(a) identification of the sources of noise;
(b) identification of steps to reduce noise levels by engineering means;
(c) establishing priorities for action;
(d) ensuring that the appropriate action is actually taken and
(e) re-assessing that effective reductions in noise exposure have been achieved.

Priorities will obviously relate to the numbers of employees concerned; the levels of exposure (concentrating on the highest exposure levels first); focussing upon the most cost-effective measures earlier rather than later, and attempting to avoid reliance upon personal ear protection wherever the working environment is hostile because of hot, humid and dirty conditions.

It should be noted that the significant qualification of the duty lies in the phrase "are likely to be exposed". Employees *do not actually have to be exposed* to the prescribed levels for the duty to arise.

It is also worth emphasising that there is a statutory embargo on the indiscriminate provision of personal protection *until* other more satisfactory and reliable engineering controls have been applied and have been found to be inadequate by themselves to bring the exposure down to the appropriate level.

Much useful advice on noise reduction methods will be found in the HSE's "Noise Guide No 4: Engineering control of noise".

Daily personal noise exposure can be reduced to some extent by restricting the time spent in noisy areas, but it should be realised that such a measure has only limited effect. For example, halving the time of exposure only reduces the daily personal noise dose by 3dB(A). Some respite from noise gives those wearing ear protection a break and is worth considering, even though the effect upon the dose is not very great.

Judging what is "reasonably practicable" where the noise exposure is constant and easily measurable is one thing, but trying to measure the exposure of those whose jobs vary from day to day and from hour to hour is much more difficult.

The role of long term programmes of plant and machinery replacement where those creating excessive noise are gradually taken out of service and new, quieter ones put in their place, is clearly going to have a major impact upon the levels of workplace noise in the future.

Ear protection

The employer's duty under NAW (Regulation 8) to provide suitable and efficient personal ear protectors is a two-stage affair:

(a) When any employee *is likely to be exposed* to noise at or above 85dB(A) (ie the first action level) in circumstances where the daily personal noise exposure *is likely to be less than 90dB(A),* the employer has to ensure, so far as is reasonably practicable, that employees are provided with suitable and efficient personal ear protectors *if they request them*.

In the 1987 consultative document the proposal was that the employer should take "all reasonable steps", but

43

in the final wording the more usual formula of words has been used.

   Some find this requirement anomalous, contending that if there is a hazard at 85dB(A) ear protection should be compulsory. Until the promised 1994 review is undertaken there is unlikely to be any change.

(b) When any employee *is likely to be exposed* to noise at or above 90dB(A) (ie the second action level), or to the peak action level (ie 200 pascals) or above, the employer must ensure, so far as is reasonably practicable, that each such employee is provided with suitable personal ear protectors. When properly worn, the ear protectors must "reasonably be expected to keep the risk of damage to the employee's hearing to *below that arising from exposure to the second action level or, as the case may be, to the peak action level*".

On the question of the choice of a suitable ear protector, reference should be made to the HSE "Noise Guide No 5: Types and selection of personal ear protectors".

   Factors affecting the suitability of the protection include:

(a) the level of noise exposure and its nature;

(b) the environment in which the protection will have to be worn;

(c) the job those having to wear the ear protection are undertaking;

(d) the suitability of the ear protectors when worn with other personal protective equipment such as goggles or respiratory protection such as respirators or breathing apparatus;

(e) the way the protectors fit the wearer and

(f) any difficulty or discomfort the wearer may experience.

When the words "provide" or "provision" are used in regulations they mean something rather more than just having the equipment on the premises. To provide something by law the employer must not only have the range of sizes and styles that will accommodate all those who may have to use the protection, but he or she must also inform those concerned where the equipment is kept, how to get it, how to look after it and keep it clean, how to ensure that it is being worn correctly, to whom defects should be reported and so on. In the case of hearing protection, hygiene matters also have to be considered. This is especially true where the type of protection chosen is in the form of ear plugs. In any cases where individuals have ear troubles involving irritation or discharge, then medical opinion should be sought before this particular type of ear protection is used.

Where individuals have a highly variable noise exposure the worst case exposure should determine the calibre of the protection used. The task of ensuring that the individuals know when and where to use their protection is of particular importance.

Ear protection zones

To indicate where, at any workplace, there are areas where the exposure of any employee to noise is *likely to be* at or above 90dB(A), or at the peak action level of 200 pascals or above, the employer is under a duty to demarcate and identify them in a specific way. Such areas are designated as "ear protection zones". The way the areas have to be identified is laid down by reference to the Safety Signs Regulations 1980 (SI 1980 No. 1471) and to Part 1 of British Standard 5378:1980.

The sign to be used is illustrated below. The symbol appears in white on a circular blue background.

Fig 10 Sign for informing that ear protectors must be worn

45

The text used with the sign must indicate that the demarcated area is an ear protection zone and that any employee entering such a demarcated zone should wear ear protection as long as he or she remains there.

The employer has to ensure, so far as is reasonably practicable, that all who go into the demarcated zones wear their ear protectors. To ensure that no doubt exists about the boundaries of an ear protection zone the signs will need to be prominently displayed at all entrances to the zones and repeated as necessary within the zones themselves.

The employer's duty to ensure, so far as is reasonably practicable, that none of his or her employees enters any ear protection zone without wearing ear protectors is contained in NAW, Regulation 9.

Maintenance of equipment

Every employer has a duty, again qualified by the phrase "so far as is reasonably practicable", to ensure that anything that he or she provides to effect compliance with the duties set out in the regulations *is fully and properly used*" (Regulation 10).

Furthermore, anything provided by the employer under the regulations must be "maintained in an efficient state, in efficient working order and in good repair" (Regulation 10 (1) (6)).

HSE guidance counsels regular checks of noise control equipment and prompt action to remedy any deficiencies found. To enable this to be done effectively it is clearly desirable that every employee is familiar with the procedure by which he or she can report anything untoward that he or she finds.

Employees' rights and duties

As has already been mentioned, employees have a right to request suitable and efficient ear protectors when they are likely to be exposed at a daily personal noise exposure of 85dB(A).

The need for employees to be convinced about the value of wearing appropriate ear protection is part of the challenge to the employer and one which is embodied in the employer's duty under Regulation 11 to impart "adequate information, instruction and training" on, amongst other things, the risk of damage to employees' hearing when exposed to the first action level (ie 85dB(A)0) and what steps can be taken to minimise that risk.

The significance of the difference between exposure to noise at 85dB(A) and 90dB(A) for the employee is a legal one. Whereas at the first action level of 85dB(A) the employee is given a right to request ear protectors from his or her employer (with a corresponding duty upon the employer to provide them) the employee is not at that level of exposure under any statutory duty to wear them.

When, however, the second action level of 90dB(A) applies, the employee has an obligation by law, so far as is reasonably practicable, to use "fully and properly" the personal ear protectors provided by his or her employer.

Any other protective measures provided by the employer to meet the requirements of NAW also have to be used "fully and properly" by employees, and they are under an obligation to report to their employer at once any defects they discover.

Because of the undoubted reluctance of some people to wear ear protection for a wide variety of reasons, from unsuitable fit to discomfort in hot and dirty environments, the HSE guidance advises "Employers should have a systematic programme to maintain usage, taking into account the following elements". The programme elements mentioned include:

(a) a commitment in the company safety policy to personal hearing protection;
(b) a positive awareness policy utilising signs and warning notices (note: this is additional to the legally required demarcation of "ear protection zones" by the provision of signs required by Regulation 9.);
(c) the identification by the employer of those responsible for the ear protection programme, and the distribution and maintenance of protectors;
(d) the acknowledgement of the training duties set out in Regulation 11;
(e) the keeping of records about the issue of protectors, arrangements for ensuring users know where and how to use them, and any problems encountered in their use.

The final element merits a separate mention and emphasis. The ear protection programme should always contain an element of monitoring. This should include, suggests HSE, spot checks to find out whether protectors are being used. "A record should be kept, and deficiencies reported to a person with responsibility and authority for remedial action."

Where employees are found not to be wearing ear protection they should be asked why. The difficulty should be resolved or a verbal warning given and recorded. "Where people persistently fail to use protectors properly they should be given a written warning and normal disciplinary procedures should be followed."

Provision of information to employees

Perhaps the most important single requirement which will guarantee the success, or otherwise, of the NAW regulations is the one requiring the employer to provide employees with adequate information, instruction and training.

Regulation 11 spells out the training syllabus in so far as it lists four topics which the employer has a duty to explain to his or her employees. The duty applies where employees are exposed to 85dB(A) or above, or to the peak action level or above (ie 200 pascals).

The four topics are:

(a) the risk of damage to hearing when an exposure of 85dB(A) or 200 pascals or above is encountered;
(b) what steps the employee can take to minimise that risk;
(c) the steps the employee must take to obtain ear protectors and
(d) the employee's legal obligations under NAW.

The extent and nature of any training will vary enormously according to the circumstances, but so long as the employees concerned actually understand the way noise can bring about insidious deterioration in their sense of hearing, the requirements will be met. It is always possible, of course, that there may be employees who either cannot read or whose native language is not English. In such cases special arrangements have to be made.

Under the Safety Representatives and Safety Committees Regulations 1977 employers are bound to make certain information available to representatives appointed under the regulations. Records of noise assessments (described in detail later in the chapter) are documents which the safety representatives are now entitled to inspect.

Noise assessments and assessment records

The Noise at Work Regulations 1989 are quite meaningless without the assessment of noise exposure. This is why there is a duty on every employer to ensure that a competent person makes an adequate noise assessment when any of his or her employees *is likely to be exposed to 85dB(A) or above, or to 200 pascals or above* (Regulation 4).

The first question an employer must answer is how does one know that one is under a duty to make an assessment before one has made an assessment? In other words, if a duty arises only when there is a likelihood of exceeding certain levels of noise exposure, how can one know whether one has any duty without knowing what level of noise exposure is involved?

The guidance offered by the Health and Safety Executive on this point is as follows – "A preliminary decision on whether an assessment is needed can usually be reached without making detailed noise measurements".

This is backed up by the following "rough guide". An assessment of daily personal exposure will usually be needed "wherever people have to shout or have difficulty being heard clearly by someone 2 metres away, or they find it difficult to talk to each other".

The purpose of a noise assessment

The employer's competent noise assessor is charged with doing two things for the purposes of NAW:

(a) identifying the employees likely to be exposed to 85dB(A) or above or to 200 pascals or above, and

(b) providing such information about noise that will enable the employer to comply with the duties imposed in relation to:
  (i) reduction of noise exposure (Regulation 7),
  (ii) ear protection (Regulation 8),
  (iii) ear protection zones (Regulation 9) and
  (iv) informing, instructing and training employees about risks from noise exposure; steps to be taken to minimise those risks; steps the employees must take to obtain ear protectors where these are appropriate; and the employees' obligations under the regulations (Regulation 11).

Competent persons

The competent person, whilst not necessarily having to make all measurements personally, will nevertheless have to be capable of analysing what information is gathered, and make a judgement upon it so that the employer is able to take all the necessary remedial measures to protect his or her employees.

"The competent person will need to be capable of not only measuring noise but of bringing together and presenting enough information about noise exposure to enable the employer to make correct decisions on what should be done to comply with the Regulations, or of advising whether additional specialist support is needed. Knowledge alone will not be sufficient; the person should possess experience and skill appropriate to the situations to be handled. The skills and knowledge will include:

(a) the purpose of assessments;
(b) an appreciation of his or her own limitations, whether of knowledge, experience, facilities or resources;
(c) how to record results and explain them to others;
(d) the reasons for using various kinds of instrument and their limitations;
(e) how to interpret information provided by others, for example on the noise generated by tools and the jobs done with them, to calculate probable exposures".

The above is an extract from HSE Noise Guide No. 1 "Legal duties of employers to prevent damage to hearing". It is further supplemented on the subject of competent persons and their role by Noise Guide No. 6 "Training for competent persons" (see the Bibliography on pages 98-9 for details of all HSE Noise Guides).

Assessment records

The noise assessments made by the competent person have to be recorded (Regulation 5).

The NAW Regulations require that the employer ensures that an "adequate record" is kept of all noise assessments and of any review of the original assessment made as a result of any *significant changes* in the work pattern.

All employers are under a duty to review their noise assessments whenever there is any reason to suspect their validity. Records for which there is no prescribed format should be kept in a "readily retrievable and easily understood form" and only need to be kept until they are superseded by a later assessment record. Despite there being no statutory requirement to keep a record of a former assessment beyond the time when a more up-to-date assessment is undertaken, it is suggested that long-term records have a value and that employers would be prudent to keep them.

Although there is no prescribed format for a record form covering a noise assessment, an example of a suitable format is set out in Fig 11. Records should at least cover the items set out in the example and provide:

(a) a tabular record of the noise exposure from various sources identified by the person or persons exposed, work area, and/or job;

(b) a plan mapping noise levels at various places, with an indication of who is exposed and the time of duration of exposure;

(c) a record of the type of location only visited occasionally, with an indication of associated noise levels and exposures.

Name and address of premises, department, etc

_____

_____

_____

Date of survey ——————— Survey made by ———————

_____

Workplace/ number of persons exposed	Noise level (Leq(s) or sound level)	Daily exposure period	$L_{EP,d}$ dB(A)	Peak pressure (where appropriate)	Comments/ remarks

General comments ————————————————————

_____

Instruments used ——————————————————————

Date of last calibration ——————————————

Signature ———————

Date ———————

Fig 11 Record of noise exposure

Fig 12 Sign suitable for warning that action is needed on an installation

Miscellaneous provisions

A number of other provisions appear in the regulations which, whilst not central to the protection of the hearing of employees exposed to noise, are necessary for the regulations' smooth functioning.

(a) The Health and Safety Executive is given powers to exempt from certain requirements under certain circumstances, if it is satisfied that the health and safety of persons likely to be affected by the exemption will not be prejudiced in consequence of it.

(b) The requirements relating to noise in the Woodworking Machines Regulations 1974 (Regulation 44) are revoked and the new regulations now apply to woodworking machines in the same way as any others.

(c) The Secretary of State for Defence may, in the interests of national security, exempt by written certificate, members of Her Majesty's Forces, visiting forces, or any

53

member of a visiting force working in, or attached to, any HQ or organisation.

The exemption may be granted subject to conditions, but before the Secretary of State for Defence grants any exemption he or she must be satisfied that suitable arrangements have been made for assessment of the health risk created by noise exposure for those subject to the exemption and for the adequate control of such noise exposure.

Modifications of manufacturers' duties

In the case of articles for use at work, or articles of fairground equipment, NAW sets out certain duties for those who supply such articles (Regulation 12).

The duty is achieved by a modification to the provisions of s. 6 of the Health and Safety at Work, etc Act 1974. The duties on manufacturers, etc (the "etc" covers designers, manufacturers, importers and suppliers) now include a requirement, where any article is likely to cause any employee to be exposed to 85dB(A) or above, or to 200 pascals or above, to provide adequate information concerning the noise likely to be generated by that article.

Those to whom the duty applies will find ample guidance on what needs to be done in HSE's Noise Guide No. 2 : "Legal duties of designers, manufacturers, importers and suppliers to prevent damage to hearing".

A removable sign for machines which produce high noise levels in some modes of use, warning that a noise survey will be needed after installation on the purchaser's premises is given in Figure 12.

An action summary of employers' legal duties is to be found in Figure 13.

Fig 13 Noise at Work Regulations, 1989
Action Summary – Legal Duties of Employers

	ALL EMPLOYERS	FIRST ACTION LEVEL	SECOND ACTION LEVEL	PEAK ACTION LEVEL
	$L_{EP,d}$ LESS THAN 85dB(A)	$L_{EP,d}$ 85dB(A)	$L_{EP,d}$ 90dB(A)	PEAK SOUND PRESSURE 200 PASCALS
Reduce hearing damage risk to lowest level reasonably practicable (Reg. 6)	*	*	*	*
Ensure competent person makes a noise assessment (Reg. 4) and keep adequate record (Reg. 5)		*	*	*
Reduce noise exposure so far as is reasonably practicable (other than by ear protectors) (Reg. 7)			*	*
Provide personal ear protectors on request (Reg. 8 (1))		*		
Ensure suitable personal ear protectors are provided (Reg. 8 (2))			*	*
Identify Ear Protection Zones (Reg. 9)			*	*
Provide adequate information instruction and training (Reg. 11)		*	*	*

European directive

The EC directive on the Protection of Workers from the Risks Related to Exposure to Noise at Work (86/188/EEC) was, as mentioned earlier, adopted on 12.5.86.

It laid down in its 14 Articles the principles to be followed in the European Community, and required that the Member States (with the exception of Greece and Portugal) should bring about the necessary changes to their domestic legislation by 1.1.90. In the cases of Greece and Portugal the relevant date was 1.1.91. In the light of progress made in scientific knowledge and technology, as well as experience gained in the implementation of the directive by Member States, there will be a re-examination of the directive before 1.1.94.

The Council, on that occasion, will try to lay down indications for measuring noise which are more precise than the ones currently given in Annex 1 of the directive. Article 7 of the directive stipulates that workers exposed to a level of 85dB(A) should be able to have their hearing checked by a doctor and, if judged necessary by the doctor, by a specialist. The way the check is carried out will follow the national law and practice of Member States.

The United Kingdom view is that medical checks, such as described above, are available through the National Health Service. The question of audiometry is not part of the statutory regime as presently envisaged, but is a matter for individual employers to determine for themselves.

The costs and benefits

Governments require economic assessments to be made when new legislation is proposed. The 1987 Consultative Document was no exception, and put forward some facts and figures before concluding that the overall costs could not be considered disproportionate to the substantial benefits associated with the new proposals for changes in the law controlling workplace noise.

Initial assessments would cost about £8.5 million, and the present value of the future recurrent cost over 40 years was estimated to be of the order of £21 million.

The cost of a personal protection programme, plus the cost

of providing information and training, could be, on average, about £12 per worker per year. It was thought that some 620,000 additional workers could be involved in expenditure under the new regulations. This could cost £7 million in the first year, and £127 million over a 40 year period at present day values.

It was assumed that it would be reasonably practicable to reduce noise at source significantly, initially in 10% of cases, rising to perhaps 50% after 40 years, at an average cost of £500 – £1000 per exposed worker. This would cost £30 – £60 million in the first year.

Benefits would accrue because fewer workers would sustain noise-induced hearing loss. If this is looked at in terms of the amount by which court compensation awards are reduced, because of the smaller number of claims, the estimated saving would be £171 – 218 million. Other savings arise from some reduction in loss of future output potential, but this is not quantifiable. On the other hand, NHS costs involved in the provision of hearing aids, a figure which is quantifiable, are likely to be £4 million.

Common law

Claims for noise-induced hearing loss attributable to noise exposure at work are dealt with in the courts in the same way as other claims for personal injuries. Persons suffering the hearing loss must establish that their employer was in breach of the duty of care towards them to take reasonable care of their hearing. Only foreseeable hazards can be the subject of negligence claims, so the first thing a plaintiff has to do is to establish that there is a risk to his or her hearing from exposure to too much noise at an employer's premises for too long a period.

"Noise and the Worker" 1963

The courts now accept that since the publication of an official guidance booklet "Noise and the Worker" in 1963, employers have been put on notice of the risk of injury to hearing where exposure to noise is established. It is unlikely now that the noise hazard will be disputed, so it is then a matter of the plaintiff establishing that he or she has been exposed to excessive noise, and that this exposure has been for a long enough period to cause hearing loss.

The 1963 booklet's section on "The Danger Levels of Noise" included a table showing a maximum sound level in dB(A) and a corresponding exposure duration in hours per day. The figures were for an 8 hour exposure 90dB(A); for 4 hours 93dB(A); for 2 hours 96dB(A); for 1 hour 99dB(A); for $^1/_2$ hour 102dB(A); and for $^1/_4$ hour 105dB(A). Later on in the section appears the statement:

> For the present it is recommended that such discrete impulses should be first assessed using an ordinary sound level meter set to the fast response, and *if the meter needle passes 90dB(A) the noise should be regarded as potentially hazardous* and should be further assessed by a specialist capable of interpreting the latest scientific literature on the subject.

In theory, both exposure to a hazardous noise level and exposure to such a level for a period long enough to cause hearing loss have to be established by the plaintiff for him or her to succeed. In practice, however, it appears that, where the level of exposure is established as potentially hazardous, the duration tends not to be a critical issue and the plaintiff succeeds, almost regardless of the period of exposure.

At this stage, what has to be reviewed are the steps, if any, taken by the employer to safeguard his or her employees' hearing. What did the employer provide either in the way of enclosures or accoustic measures, or personal protective equipment to mitigate the hazard? The word "provide", as intimated earlier, is interpreted narrowly. The employer really has to have the protective equipment available at the point where the hazard is encountered. He or she also has to inform, instruct and train those exposed to the hazard in what they should do to protect themselves, and a disciplinary regime should exist to enforce this. This is now part of the NAW regime required by Regulation 11.

The final matter which the plaintiff has to tackle is to show that the loss of hearing he or she suffered came about as a result of the defendant employer's negligence. This is a matter of medical history and of investigating whether the plaintiff has been exposed to other sources of injurious noise which could explain the condition. These could include gun shots from shooting sports, or explosions during the course of hostilities, etc. If the plaintiff can establish that such exposures were suffered, he or she will succeed, on the balance of probabilities, in establishing the defendant employer's negligence and be awarded damages.

Cases of significance

It may be helpful at this juncture to make reference to three significant cases relevant to the subject of employees whose hearing has been affected by noise at their place of work.

Paris' case

Where a duty is owed by one person to another, such as by an employer to one of his or her employees, the duty is owed to each employee as an individual. The discharge of the duty must take into account individual peculiarities which are known, or which ought to be known, to the employer. In the Paris case what ought to have been known was that a man with one eye, such as Mr Paris, ran a greater risk of blindness than a normally sighted person. Paris's employer failed to take note of this when the question of eye protection was at issue.

It is submitted that following this precedent it is important for an employer to know, and to record, the state of hearing of new employees when he or she takes them on, because the duty of care will be greater towards those taken on who may already have suffered some measurable degree of hearing loss, irrespective of its cause or causes. The above comments should be read together with those on audiometry on pages 29-31.

In a House of Lords case, approving the decision in the Paris case, Lord Morton said "the more serious the damage which will happen if an accident occurs, the more thorough are the precautions which an employer must take". It is submitted that the principle applies just as much in the case of workplace noise-induced hearing loss, as in the case of an accident. The principle was summed up in the same case by Lord Oaksey when he said "The duty of an employer towards his servant is to take reasonable care for his servant's safety *in all the circumstances of the case*". Part of the relevant circumstances in the Paris case included the fact that Mr Paris only had one good eye so that the consequence of anything untoward happening to it were bound to be more serious to him than to a man with two eyes (*Paris v Stepney Borough Council* [1951] AC367, [1951] 1 All ER 42).

Berry's Case

With good hearing Mr Frank Richard Berry began to work at Stone Manganese Marine Limited (SMM Ltd) in 1957.

He was exposed to noise levels of between 115–120dB(A).

His employers provided no ear muffs until 1966, but had earlier provided ear plugs in two out of a range of seven available sizes. The plugs stocked by SMM Ltd afforded insufficient protection against the noise levels to which Mr Berry was exposed at its premises.

By 1960 Mr Berry realised that the noise to which he was exposed at his workplace was affecting his hearing, but he did not consult a doctor until 1964. Nothing happened following this first consultation.

In 1967 Mr Berry again consulted his doctor. This time the doctor sent Mr Berry to a consultant surgeon. An audiogram was taken in November 1967 following this consultation.

In February 1968 Mr Berry consulted his trade union about the deterioration in his hearing. In April 1970 Mr Berry was given leave to bring an action for damages for negligence against SMM Ltd. Mr Berry's employer claimed that such an action was time-barred, which simply meant that it was alleged Mr Berry was too late in bringing his claim before the court.

Mr Berry claimed that SMM Ltd was negligent in not having his hearing tested by audiometry and that accordingly he was entitled to full damages because the damage to his hearing was caused by negligence in the three years immediately preceding the issue of the writ.

Mr Justice Ashworth gave judgment for Mr Berry and held that:

(a) the defendant (SMM Ltd) was negligent from the time when the plaintiff (Mr Berry) began to work for the firm because it had not sought advice, and had not supplied more than two sizes of ear plugs, and had not provided supervision over their selection. The company was also negligent in not supplying ear muffs. Because, said Mr Justice Ashworth, with adequate propaganda, Mr Berry would probably have worn them from the outset.

(b) the defendant was not negligent in failing to arrange for the plaintiff's hearing to be tested by audiometry, for its duty as an employer did not involve taking steps to discover whether an employee's hearing was being affected.

(c) Mr Berry's claim in respect of matters arising more than three years before the writ was issued was statute-barred because the long story of increasing deafness, due to inadequate protection of his hearing, would have led any reasonable man to seek advice before 1967. Mr Berry had not done so.

(d) the defendant's negligence in not taking steps to encourage or persuade the wearing of ear muffs continued after 1967 while Mr Berry's hearing became worse as a result. He was therefore entitled to reasonable compensation for the increase in loss which could be determined on the evidence of the audiograms and his own evidence, giving sufficient weight to the fact that making a man already deaf even deafer was to increase his handicap considerably.

It is interesting to learn of Mr Justice Ashworth's comments at the conclusion of his judgment in the Berry case. He said that if he had to award Mr Berry damages for his deafness at the time of the judgment, and also to compensate him for all the discomfort he had suffered since 1960, he would have awarded him £2500.

He concluded, however, that he only had to compensate him for the deterioration suffered since April 1967. "It would not be right to base an award merely on arithmetic, and calculate it as being four-elevenths of the total sum, on the footing that he has had eleven years of deafness and only four of them since April 1967. Such a course would not give sufficient weight to the fact that to make a man already deaf still deafer is to increase his handicap very considerably: as Dr Coles (a medical expert witness in the case) said, he has fewer decibels to spare."

Judgment was given to Mr Berry in the sum of £1250 (*Berry v Stone Manganese Marine Limited* [1971] 115 Sol Jo 966, [1972] 1 Lloyd's Rep 182).

Note: Berry's case related to work in a chipping shop where manganese bronze propellers were shaped by the use of pneumatic hammers. Several men in the chipping shop were using pneumatic tools at the same time. The noise was "bordering on the threshold of pain" according to one of the witnesses who gave evidence at the hearing.

McCafferty's case

Whereas the Berry case involved a fairly continuous and sustained exposure to high noise levels from pneumatic tools, the McCafferty case concerned exposure to regular but occasional high-impact noise (see pages 28-9).

The plaintiff was a detective inspector in the police force and in 1948 was appointed liaison officer for the police laboratory at Scotland Yard. Soon afterwards he began helping with experimental work on firearms which was carried out in the laboratory under the supervision of scientists. In due time he became a leading expert on ballistics. His work involved him conducting shooting tests on firearms used in connection with criminal offences, and then giving evidence in court on the results of his investigations. At the end of 1964 he retired from the police force but was re-employed by the Receiver for the Metropolitan Police District as a member of the civilian staff. Under the control of the laboratory director he was put in charge of the ballistics section of the laboratory.

In September 1965 the ballistics section moved to new premises. Although intended to be a temporary move, the laboratory remained there until 1974. In 1965 Mr McCafferty undertook shooting tests in connection with approximately 200 cases. In the years that followed the number of cases increased by about 20 per cent annually.

The room where tests were carried out was 22 feet by 6 feet and not equipped with sound absorbent walls, curtains or other sound absorbent material to protect his hearing against the noise made by the discharge of firearms in a confined space. Scientists in the laboratory led McCafferty to believe that cotton wool placed in the ears would provide adequate protection from the noise associated with his work. He used cotton wool until 1967 when a doctor told him that the cotton wool offered no protection and that he should wear ear-muffs. He immediately asked the director for ear muffs and these were promptly supplied. They were not, however, as effective as they should have been because he did not wear them in the correct manner.

At the end of 1967 Mr McCafferty noticed that the ringing in his ears (tinnitus) persisted for longer than usual after he had been discharging firearms as part of his job. He saw a specialist who took an audiogram and diagnosed a hearing defect resulting from acoustic trauma. The specialist did not consider that there would be further deterioration if Mr McCafferty continued to wear ear muffs correctly.

The plaintiff (Mr McCafferty) did not tell the director about his hearing defect because he regarded the tinnitus as ''an irritating nuisance''. He did not take any legal action against the Receiver for failing to provide adequate acoustic protection in the room where he worked with firearms. The senior architectural assistant in the Receiver's department knew by this time, however, that the room required sound-proofing, but took no remedial action.

In 1969 the specialist who Mr McCafferty saw reported no further significant change in his hearing since 1967. Mr McCafferty did not notice any change in his hearing between 1967 and 1973 and made no complaint to his superiors about the lack of acoustic protection in the room. In 1973 it was decided to have routine audiograms taken of certain police personnel. Mr McCafferty's audiogram showed signs of severe acoustic trauma and he was advised to stop working at once. His employment was prematurely terminated in October 1973 when he was 58.

It was discovered later when another audiogram was taken in 1975 that there had been no substantial change in Mr McCafferty's hearing between 1967 and 1975, allowing for his age and that the trauma indicated in 1973 was only a temporary one caused by the noise of a shot or series of shots in the few days before the 1973 audiogram had been taken.

In January 1974 Mr McCafferty issued a writ against the Receiver on the grounds that his hearing had been seriously damaged by the end of 1967 (the first incident), and his career brought to a premature end in 1973 (the second incident) as a result of the Receiver's failure to take reasonable measures to protect him against the danger to his hearing while working in the firearms room. The Receiver knew, or ought to have known, that there was danger from the noise.

The Receiver denied negligence and contended that even if the plaintiff had developed tinnitus as a result of inadequate acoustic protection in the room, Mr McCafferty had caused or contributed to it by his own negligence since the director had delegated to him the task of making enquiries about the safety requirements for the new room. The defendant said that the claim in relation to the first incident was time-barred because it had not been brought within three years of the date when he knew of the injury and its probable cause.

At the hearing the judge held that the first incident was caused by the plaintiff's exposure to noise and the second incident was caused by insufficient acoustic protection at the workplace. He held that the Receiver had been negligent, that the plaintiff had not been guilty of contributory negligence, and that the plaintiff's claim was not time-barred. He awarded Mr McCafferty £850 damages in respect of the first incident and £9150 in respect of the second incident.

The Receiver appealed but the appeal was dismissed.

The Court of Appeal held that the employer (the Receiver) had failed to discharge his duty as a careful employer to take reasonable care to protect the plaintiff from the foreseeable risk of danger to his health in respect of both incidents involving exposure to noise from the discharge of firearms. The Receiver should have taken competent advice. Had he done so he would have found that ear muffs and some form of sound proofing were necessary and that the plaintiff would have been protected from further deterioration of his hearing. It was no defence to say that the plaintiff had made no complaint. Nor was it acceptable for the Receiver to delegate the making of enquiries to the plaintiff.

The Court of Appeal also held that Mr McCafferty was not guilty of any contributory negligence in respect of the first incident. He could not be blamed for believing that cotton wool provided adequate protection since he had been told by scientists that it did afford him adequate protection.

As far as the second incident was concerned, again Mr McCafferty was not guilty of contributory negligence because he did not have sufficient awareness of the risk of damage, and of the degree of protection afforded by acoustic protection. He had been led to believe that ear muffs provided sufficient protection. The Court of Appeal also held that the claim made by Mr McCafferty was not time-barred in respect of the first incident (*McCafferty v Metropolitan Police District Receiver* [1972] 2 All ER 756).

From a reading of the above cases it will have been observed that the majority of the key points raised have been covered by the new Noise at Work Regulations and their accompanying Noise Guides.

Damages

Damages awarded to successful plaintiffs in industrial deafness cases vary according to a number of factors: age; degree of hearing loss; life-style; existence of accompanying disabilities such as tinnitus; and, sometimes, loss of earnings.

The following cases illustrate the wide range in the amount of damages awarded:

(a) 1979, moderately severe deafness and tinnitus, £7,500;
(b) 1981, severe deafness and tinnitus, loss of earnings, £15,000;
(c) 1982, deafness and loss of amenity cases, £2,500 – £6,500;
(d) 1990, four workers at a factory making motor cars were awarded £24,500 damages between them because they had been partially deafened at work. The awards amounted to £7,500; £6,500; £6,000 and £4,500 respectively, reflecting the degree of hearing loss in each case.

An estimate from a solicitor specialising in deafness cases puts the worth of claims actually reaching the courts as ranging from £2,500 – £15,000.

Increasingly, employers, through their insurers, are party to an agreement with the relevant Trades Union to which their employees belong. Such agreements, known as Scheme Agreements, have a sliding scale of compensation varying from a £300 award for a 60 year-old man with a hearing loss of

10-14dB up to £11,000 for a 40 year-old man with a hearing loss of up to 96dB.

Contributory negligence

Employees have both statutory and common law duties to protect themselves. If they fail to fulfil their statutory duty they commit a criminal offence and the courts can fine them. If they fail to fulfil their common law duty to protect themselves, there will be a finding of contributory negligence against them and the damages awarded to them will be reduced to an extent commensurate with their own negligence. This is a matter determined by the judge after he or she has considered all the circumstances of the particular case.

Often the issue of contributory negligence turns upon the question of the condoning of a bad practice by an employer. If, for example, a foreman fitter knows that one of his staff goes regularly into a noisy compressor house without ear protectors, and the foreman has taken no steps to enforce the use of the protective equipment by the fitter, the latter will be able to say the failure to use the protectors was condoned by the foreman. The employers, because they are vicariously liable for their foreman's act of condoning the fitter's failure to use hearing protection, will not succeed in convincing the court that the fitter was negligent. In the event, however, the full damages would probably not be awarded because the fitter would almost certainly be unable to deny, during cross-examination, that he or she was completely unaware of the existence of the risks from the hazard of noise, and that ear protectors should have been worn.

When the demarcation of ear protection zones becomes obligatory, it will be more difficult for employees to deny that they were unaware of the hazards to which their attention is constantly being drawn by notices. Nevertheless, much will still depend upon the attitude of the employer, especially at the workplace itself where any condoning of bad practices begins with shopfloor supervision.

Now that the employer has duties to inform, instruct and train his or her employees and to identify and demarcate ear protection zones (where by definition there is likely to be a noise level of 90dB(A) or above), he or she will be able to establish contributory negligence more easily by reference to procedures set up to achieve compliance with NAW. Similarly, the employee may be more easily able to deny contributory negligence when he or she can show the employer's procedures required under NAW to be lacking.

Chapter 4

Noise control

A number of options exist to control noise at source. Efficient routine maintenance should eliminate sources such as loose machine parts, and air and steam leaks. Substitution, re-design, and re-siting may prove to be effective measures. Further control methods include the use of vibration isolators, insulation, absorption, silencers and sound havens.

When noise is excessive, the ideal response is to reduce it. Provided it stays reduced, the problems of providing and enforcing the wearing of ear protection, ear protection zones, and so on disappear.

However, noise reduction can be expensive and complicated. It is sometimes impossible. This chapter will review the main options available, without going into the depth of technical detail which is the province of the specialist publications given in the bibliography.

The survey

It is not uncommon to find that the introduction of expensive noise control measures comes as a disappointment to all concerned because the noise reduction is much less than was anticipated. The reason for this is that one particular noise source has been tackled, but another one now dominates. It is thus essential that before any noise control is introduced, a proper noise survey is undertaken. The survey should identify all significant noise sources and should be used to predict the effect on the overall level of noise reduction alternatives.

Basic measures

Another action to undertake at an early stage is to ensure that all readily controlled noises are eliminated. Major offenders here are air and steam leaks. These can produce a high frequency background noise to which everyone becomes resigned, but which can be removed by simple engineering measures, backed up by adequate routine maintenance.

A further common source is the rattling and drumming of machine parts which are not securely fastened. For example, bolted sections of machine guards can work loose and then set up an incessant vibration which becomes one of the major causes of workplace noise. The solution is obvious, but until such basic engineering measures are undertaken, the devising of sophisticated noise control devices is pointless.

Sometimes, impacts can be avoided or "damped". This may be achieved with rubber buffers, surface coatings on chutes to prevent metal to metal impacts, and use of conveyor systems which prevent items rattling together. Machine parts which "ring" can often be damped with surface coatings or constructed from a number of bolted items rather than a single welded unit.

Substitution

If workplace noise arises primarily from a small number of identifiable sources, say noisy machines, then an ideal solution would be change the machines for quieter ones. Noise control technology has advanced considerably in recent years and equipment manufacturers have been under considerable pressure to minimise noise output. It is therefore likely that a less noisy version is now available and that the supplier will be able to specify the noise output which can be expected. If such data is not provided because NAW requires it, it should certainly be requested.

If substitution could theoretically solve a noise problem, the overriding objection is likely to be the cost.

The cost of replacing high capital value items may rule out this option, but it is worth ensuring that the cost analysis has taken all factors into account. These might include, for example, the possible increased output from new, more efficient, machines. Also included should be the savings in the hearing protection programme (ear muffs, noise zones, audiometry, etc) which might be avoidable altogether if the noise level is reduced.

Re-design

It may not be necessary to replace a complex machine completely if a modification to its design can reduce noise. This is a specialist subject, but possible components for re-design might be the bearings or gears of rotating machinery. Bearing noise might be reduced by improved lubrication or flexible mountings. Gear re-design might include different tooth formation, or use of plastic components in the gear train.

Re-siting

An attractive approach to noise control in some locations is not to silence the machines, but to move them to where their noise is less of a problem. This might, for example, entail re-routing pipework so that components which are noisy but require only limited access, such as pumps, are located remotely from the main operating area.

An alternative might be to group noisy equipment together, accepting the fact that this will result in an area or room requiring the use of hearing protectors, but enabling other production areas to be free of such restrictions.

This has been a successful approach with equipment such as tabletting machines which can be the only noisy section in an otherwise quiet production line. By creating a separate tabletting room, the use of protective equipment is restricted to the one area, and job rotation can reduce the time which any individual must spend in the area.

Vibration isolation

If a power driven machine stands, or is fixed, directly on a hard surface, then it is likely that energy will be transmitted through the mounting points into the surrounding structure. The consequent vibration of that structure, which may of course be the floor, can be responsible for the majority of the noise arising from the machine. The solution is to isolate the machinery by inserting vibration isolators between the mounting points and the operating surface.

Vibration isolators are generally specified according to their static deflection. This is the distance which the isolator will yield under the load of the machine. The manufacturer will generally advise on the appropriate isolator for a particular machine. It is essential to seek and follow this advice since much the best results will be obtained from isolators which are accurately specified. Indeed, installation of the wrong isolators can introduce new vibration patterns which make the situation worse.

The simplest vibration isolators consist of pads of resilient material such as cork or felt. However, these do not give good isolation over a wide range of frequencies. They can also deteriorate with age, or on exposure to water and oil. For more versatile and durable application, the majority of isolators are of rubber-in-shear type consisting of a rubber body with a metal top and base. When these are specified according to their deflection the "dynamic" deflection should be known because rubber is less yielding when it is actually vibrating than when it is static.

The main remaining type of vibration isolator is the steel spring mount. These give the greatest static deflection and therefore isolate the lowest frequencies of vibration. To prevent high frequency components being transmitted through the coils of the spring, there is usually a rubber pad between the spring and the body of the isolator.

A possible consideration in installing vibration isolators is the inherent strength of the machine frame. If the frame relies for its stiffness on the support from the floor, this will be lost when the isolator is installed. It might then be necessary to mount the machine on a new frame or bed, and then to install this on the vibration isolators.

A final factor to consider is that the machine might be transmitting vibration through routes other than its base. These might include connecting pipes and services, etc. It will then be necessary to introduce flexible connectors such as rubber hose to ensure that there is no vibration bridging path left from the machine. This is most important since the value of isolators can be eliminated if bridging paths are left. Manufacturers will advise on correct specifications.

Insulation

Perhaps the most obvious approach to noise reduction is to put a box around the source in the hope that this will enclose troublesome noise. This technique of noise insulation is indeed appropriate in many circumstances but it raises a number of issues of specification and design.

The first consideration is – of what material should the box be made? There is much confusion about what constitutes a good noise insulator. This is partly because materials such as polystyrene tiles which are installed to reduce sound reflection in rooms, are also assumed to prevent noise transmission. They do not. Materials which have good insulation properties are, in the main, those which have a high density. In addition, the material should ideally have a low stiffness.

These considerations invariably result in a compromise. The ideal high density/low stiffness material would perhaps be lead. However, cost notwithstanding, lead would not be a sensible material from which to build an industrial enclosure. Brick, though not very high density, gives good insulation in the form of brick walls of usual thickness. But brick might not be practical for fabricating an in-plant enclosure. Steel, a good construction material of high density, also has a high stiffness which reduces its insulation effectiveness. It is thus common to find that a compromise consists of composite materials which give a reasonable combination of density (or mass), whilst reducing the effects of high stiffness.

For example, steel may be used which has had a damping layer of mastic applied to one side to reduce the effect of stiffness. It is also possible to find combinations of steel and plasterboard, mineral wool or lead.

Having selected a suitable material, it is necessary to design the enclosure. This is likely to be difficult because the enclosure cannot usually be a close-fitting, completely sealed box. Services must be fed into and taken out of the enclosure, as must the product. In addition, a good acoustic insulator will probably be a good heat insulator, and ventilation must be introduced which does not destroy the acoustic properties. It may also be necessary to fit doors and windows into the enclosure to permit viewing, and allow access for maintenance.

These considerations demand detailed, specialist design. It is disappointing to find that a "home made" enclosure produces nowhere near the hoped for noise reduction because insufficient attention has been given to the selection of materials, or to constructing an enclosure which has no gaps or holes through which noise could escape.

Absorption

When sound strikes a surface some of it is absorbed, some is transmitted through the material, and some is reflected. We have looked at the characteristics of good insulation materials, but in many circumstances it is desirable to minimise the sound reflection. Typical examples are the lining of a ceiling to reduce reverberant effects, and the internal lining of acoustic enclosures.

This latter feature is desirable because if sound reflection is reduced inside the enclosure, less sound will impinge on its surrounding walls to be imparted to the outside. As discussed, it is important to differentiate between the need for insulation and absorption. Insulation is required if noise is to be prevented from penetrating an occupied area from outside, or from an enclosure. Absorption is appropriate if the noise source is within a certain area and it is desired to reduce its reflection from surrounding surfaces.

Absorptive materials do not have the same high density requirements as insulators. They are usually materials with a porous surface structure such as mineral and glass fibre, and polyurethane foams. If the absorptive surface must be more durable than these materials, then perforated metal sheet is often fitted. A layer of thin, impervious plastic may also be included to prevent the ingress of oils, etc.

In some cases, where high levels of absorption are required, it is possible to space absorptive panels so that reflected sound strikes another panel and is progressively reduced. This is normally achieved by hanging panels vertically from the ceiling.

Silencers

Devices such as fans, which push air along a system of pipes or ducts frequently benefit from the installation of silencers. The objective is to reduce noise transmitted through the system, whilst retaining a reasonably free flow of air.

Most silencing of this sort uses a system of progressive absorption of the noise. This can often be achieved simply by lining the inside of the duct with suitable absorption material such as mineral wool. When silencing of low frequency noise is required, it is necessary to "split" the duct into sections, each of which has a width much smaller than its height. Splitter silencers achieve this with baffles of sound absorption material.

When silencing is required primarily at a specific frequency, it may be appropriate to use reactive silencers. These operate by forcing the air to oscillate through narrow constrictions in such a way that the sound waves coincide and cancel each other out. Reactive silencers can be tuned to the frequency to be controlled and are not effective at other frequencies. They are therefore suitable for constant speed machines generating noise at a discrete frequency.

Sound havens

If reducing machinery noise is impossible, or prohibitively expensive, it may be worth creating a quiet enclosure or haven for employees to occupy for at least part of their working day. The principles of construction of a haven are essentially those for an acoustic enclosure, except that their function is to keep noise out, rather than to keep it in.

The sound haven approach can sometimes be taken to elaborate lengths by connecting instruments and controls within the enclosure. It may then be possible for the majority of process activities to be undertaken in a quiet environment with relatively little need to enter the noisy plant areas.

Conclusion

Of necessity this has been a basic review of a technically complex subject. The main methods of noise reduction have been described, and emphasis has been placed on the importance of undertaking the simpler, cheaper options first. However, the detailed design and construction work requires specialist input, and is dealt with in the textbooks on acoustic treatment.

Chapter 5

Hearing protection

When noise can not, within the constraints of reasonable practicability, be reduced at source, the individual worker's exposure to it may be reduced by his or her use of personal protective equipment. Such equipment may be external to the ear, in the form of an earmuff, or inserted into the outer ear, in the form of a plug. Such remedial measures must be accompanied by appropriate worker instruction and motivation and the clear marking of the noise zones where such protection is necessary.

Personal protection

If noise reduction measures do not achieve the desired standard, and further reduction is technically impractical or economically unrealistic, then there will be a need to resort to personal protection. This is obviously not ideal. It would be preferable to work in a quiet environment than to suffer the inconvenience, and sometimes discomfort, of hearing protectors. Nevertheless, properly used protection devices can achieve full protection against deafness in the majority of situations. And, if carefully selected, can result in only limited discomfort.

The types of hearing protection are usually described as earmuffs or earplugs.

Earmuffs

Earmuffs consist of high-attenuation cups which fit over the ears and are held firmly in position by a steel or plastic headband. The seal around the head is achieved with a soft cushion which, in the most efficient muffs, is filled with liquid. The slight improvement in efficiency obtained from liquid-filled seals must be offset against the fact that the liquid seal will leak if damaged. All seals should be easily replaceable.

The inside of an earmuff cup is partly filled with an absorbent material to reduce resonance in the shell.

It is possible to obtain earmuffs which incorporate a facility for electronic communication: music or messages are broadcast inside the earmuff cups. This is achieved by wire connections to fixed points, or by transmission through an induction loop so that no connections are needed. This is an expensive form of protection, but may overcome the isolation that some people feel when wearing earmuffs.

Earplugs

Earplugs are plugs of soft flexible material with high sound attenuation properties, which are pushed into the entrance of the ear canal. Many earplugs are disposable and are intended to be used only once. These are usually made from cylinders of soft plastic foam, or from glass wool. The plastic foam plugs are rolled up in the fingers before insertion, and they then slowly expand to fit tightly into the ear canal. Glass wool plugs may either be preformed, or come in wads of material which the user folds into a plug. Both are commonly provided from dispenser machines fitted on the wall of the workplace.

Non-disposable earplugs are made from soft plastic or rubber. They are preformed plugs designed to fit closely in the ear canal. However, because the human ear does not come in a standard size, such plugs generally have to be available in a number of fittings.

Selection

The hearing protector is a very simple device. It is a mechanism for insulating the ear rather than the noise source. However, there is an enormous number of types and brands available and the selection of the best model requires some care. There are two considerations: the protector must suit both the workplace and the user.

The workplace

It goes without saying that the protector must cut out sufficient workplace noise to ensure that the user is at no risk of hearing damage. Ideally, this would be achieved by the attenuation of a given hearing protector being specified in A-weighted decibels. Thus, in a noisy environment of 100dB(A), we could be sure that ear plugs with at least 20dB(A) attenuation would be satisfactory (since we can reasonably assume that 80dB(A) and below does negligible damage).

Unfortunately, specifying hearing protectors with a simple dB(A) rating is not possible. The reason is that all protection devices have different efficiencies at different frequencies. In other words, a particular ear muff might be very efficient at cutting out noise at a frequency of around 1000Hz, but less effective at frequencies which are much higher or much lower. Thus, the reduction in dB(A) would be high if the noise was around 1000Hz, but lower if the noise was around, say, 100Hz.

To summarise, the degree of protection given by a particular set of hearing protectors will depend upon the frequency distribution of the workplace noise, and the particular attenuation characteristics of the protectors themselves.

Obtaining the effectiveness of a particular hearing protector at various frequencies is reasonably straightforward – the manufacturers of all reputable equipment will provide the data on request. This is likely to take the form of a graph of attenuation in decibels (not A-weighted) at varying frequencies. It is now necessary to assess whether these attenuation characteristics will give adequate protection in the area of concern. This requires a frequency analysis of the workplace noise. The effective new level (to the wearer of the protectors) is then obtained by subtracting the attenuation figure from the actual decibel level within each frequency band. This is illustrated on the graph (Fig 14). Whilst this exercise can be used to compare one hearing protector with another, it does not directly produce the effective reduction in dB(A) level and, if we are working to a dB(A) standard, this will be required. It is therefore usual to plot the figures on curves showing the A-weighted decibel levels. This will show both the effective dB(A) level to the user of the hearing protectors, as well as indicating at what frequency further attenuation will be necessary to obtain a still lower dB(A) figure.

Having compared the attenuation characteristics of various hearing protectors against the requirements of a particular workplace, there will almost certainly be a range of protectors which will be suitable.

In fact, for fairly broad band noise which is not too excessive, virtually all the hearing protectors on the market would probably be satisfactory. The choice can then be made on other factors such as availability, ease of maintenance, and cost.

Muffs or plugs?

One of the most debated issues in choosing hearing protectors is whether it is preferable to use earmuffs or earplugs. From the point of view of protection, either can be perfectly adequate in the majority of circumstances. This is said with the slight reservation that some people find it difficult to use ear plugs.

80

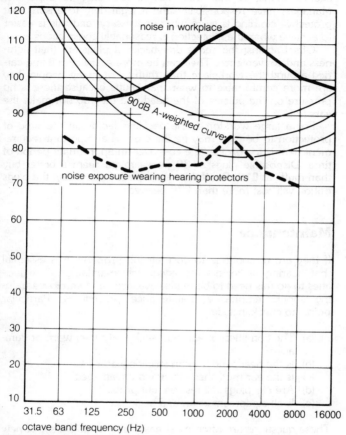

octave band level (dB)

octave band frequency (Hz)

Fig 14 Graph illustrating the attenuation achieved by hearing protectors at different frequencies.

Perhaps this results from childhood conditioning not to push anything into the ears – whatever the reason it can mean that ear plugs are perched on the outside of the ears rather than firmly pushed into position. A further drawback of plugs, as against muffs, is that their use is less easy to supervise. Managers have responsibility and a legal duty to ensure that protective clothing is worn where necessary, and this is easier to achieve when the protection is reasonably conspicuous.

Offset against the above drawbacks of plugs are their lightness and convenience. They can be more easily stored and carried around the workplace than muffs. For many people they are more comfortable to wear than muffs because there is no pressure on the outside of the head and they do not make the ears hot.

For a large workforce, the deciding factor on the type of protection to be used may be the cost. The important requirement here is to consider the cost over an appropriate period of time. Disposable plugs at 30 pence might seem a better buy than muffs at £10. But if they are replaced every day, the plugs option will cost more than £70 per year.

Maintenance

If they are to continue to do their job properly, it is essential that hearing protectors are adequately maintained. The facilities to do this need to be readily available, and employee training should emphasise maintenance procedures. Particular points to check include:

(a) The condition of ear muff seals – are they worn or damaged?
(b) Is the headband tension still adequate?
(c) Is the ear muff shell intact and undamaged?
(d) Are ear plugs still resilient but pliable?
(e) Is all equipment clean and hygienic.

These questions are often most easily answered if a set of new protectors is to hand for comparison.

Involving the workforce

Hearing protectors are amongst the more comfortable types of protective clothing for long term continuous use. However, no one would wear them from choice and an effective protection programme will require education, persuasion and assistance. The mere issue of protectors will not guarantee their use, and does not meet an employer's legal obligations. It is therefore essential that every employee who should be using hearing protectors is trained in the reasons why they are necessary, and the proper procedures for fitting them and keeping them in good order. Ideally, this exercise should include allowing a personal choice from a number of suitable alternatives.

Involvement of the workforce in the application of protective clothing is absolutely essential. However, it raises some questions which must be answered. The main ones are:

(a) *Will hearing protectors prevent communication?*
   To be heard in a noisy environment, it is necessary to shout over the background noise.

   Hearing protectors will reduce both the background noise and the shouting to the same extent and the ability to communicate remains the same. The answer is therefore that, when the noise level is over about 85 dB(A), hearing protectors do not impair the ability to communicate. However, this may psychologically be the impression, because wearing protectors creates an unusual environment for most people. The answer is to give the brain time to adjust. If the wearer can be persuaded to persevere for about two weeks, he or she will invariably find that their use becomes quite acceptable.

(b) *Can hearing protectors cause infections?*
   The concern that protectors, particularly ear plugs, might cause infection, is common. Observations over a long period of time have shown that such a risk is negligible, and that the ear is quite resistant to repeated insertion of plugs. Nevertheless, hearing protectors must be kept scrupulously clean, and employees must have adequate facilities for proper cleaning and storage.

(c) *Surely I'm immune to noise by now?*
   Employees who have already worked, perhaps for several years, in a noisy environment, can be particularly resistant to wearing hearing protectors. Their grounds are that noise can do them no further damage. It is

essential to explain to such individuals the true nature of noise-induced deafness. No resistance builds up, and noise will continue to inflict damage until deafness becomes total.

Employees who have been exposed to noise, and who may already be partially deaf, have a vital need to preserve what is left of their hearing before it is too late.

(d) *Why should we wear hearing protectors when managers don't?*

It is a good question! The fact is that many noise control programmes are undermined by the behaviour of managers and visitors. This point is emphasised below in the consideration of ear protection zones. If managers do not follow their own rules, there cannot be the slightest hope that anyone else will.

(e) *Surely it's alright to wear protectors most, but not all the time?*

Unfortunately not. In a high noise area, the unprotected ear will be at risk after a very short period of time. For example, ear muffs designed to give 30 dB(A) cf protection would give only 9 dB(A) of protection if they were left off for just one hour each day. In practice, however, it is more comfortable and convenient to wear protectors all the time rather than take them on and off. This is because we adapt to the new environment after a period of time – and find that communication, etc becomes less of a problem. However, this will only happen if we give it a chance – and leave the protectors on.

Ear protection zones

A final point on the introduction of hearing protectors. It must be quite unambiguous where they should be worn. Areas in which protectors are to be used must be clearly marked; the boundary should be a conspicuous barrier or floor marking, and notices should make it obvious to everyone that protectors are required within the zone (NAW Regulation 9).

It is sometimes said that managers and visitors who are entering the zone for only a short time, need not wearing protectors. Whilst this may be correct in terms of the noise dose received, it is totally unworkable in practice. The only way to enforce a noise protection policy is for everyone to be bound by it at all times. The alternative is interminable discussions about how long an individual has been in the zone, *etc.* In an ear protection zone, everybody *must wear hearing protectors all of the time.*

Chapter 6

Management action plan

The objective of any management hearing protection policy may be achieved by a step-by-step plan. This will include consideration of the following: surveying workplace noise; setting a standard; reduction of noise by simple obvious measures; marking noise zones; choosing and enforcing the use of hearing protectors; specifying noise limits for new equipment; audiometry; checking and reviewing progress with the overall noise control policy; and ensuring the existence of adequate records.

Action checklist

This book has so far reviewed the legal and technical background to the subject of noise-induced deafness. However, this is now a preventable condition, and managers are charged with ensuring that the likelihood of it occurring in the workplace under their control, is negligible. This final chapter is presented as an action checklist which, if implemented, will essentially prevent noise-induced deafness. In addition, it will ensure that all legal obligations relating to noise, are fulfilled.

Undertake a noise survey

As with many other problems, the solution begins with measurement. In general, it is necessary to know the dB(A) level in each working position in the workplace. However, measurements are not needed from areas which are obviously quiet. Equally, quite a number of measurements may be taken in the noisy areas. This will give an idea of variations during the day, which machines are particularly noisy, etc.

It is possible to continue the measurement exercise in great detail, repeating the survey regularly, and extending the measurements to frequency analysis, and a number of variants on the decibel. Some of this may be worthwhile. However, it is common to see excessive measurement of an occupational health problem used as a substitute for doing something about it.

Further measurement is only necessary when additional information is required, or when there is a reason to believe that noise levels might have changed.

Determine noise dose

Identification of high dB(A) levels does not necessarily prove a noise hazard since there may be very limited exposure to those levels. Thus, if noise levels vary through the day, or, if employees are moving around, the noise dose of individuals must be obtained. The figure needed is the individual's continuous noise level over the working day - the $L_{EP,d}$.

The $L_{EP,d}$ may be relatively easy to estimate on the basis that doubling the sound energy increases the dB(A) level by 3.

Thus, if an individual spends half his or her working day (4 hours) at a noise level of 95dB(A), the $L_{EP,d}$ will be 92dB(A), assuming that the rest of his or her time is spent in a quiet environment.

However, if the employee works at many different noise levels, the L_{EP} becomes virtually impossible to calculate and must be measured. This is most conveniently achieved with a personal noise dose meter which the employee "wears" throughout the day. At the end of the day, the $L_{EP,d}$ can be read off directly.

Set a standard

The first two stages of this action plan will have produced some numbers – ultimately expressed as $L_{EP,d}$ readings. It is now necessary to decide whether these findings are satisfactory, or whether action is required to reduce them. Legislation has set three action levels:

the first action level   –   an $L_{EP,d}$ of 85 dB(A)
the second action level   –   an $L_{EP,d}$ of 90 dB(A)
the peak action level   –   a peak sound pressure of 200 pascals.

The chapter on legislation explains the steps which must be taken at these action levels, and the rest of this action check list provides further advice. However, it is possible that actions may be desirable at lower levels than those set out in legislation. This is because, firstly, the noise measurements may not be accurate – an error of 3 dB(A) would not be unusual in the most commonly used industrial noise meters. Secondly, it may be desired to protect a larger proportion of the workforce than would be protected by the legal standards. However, these considerations must be set against the commercial and practical realities of the business. All these issues must be discussed and a clear standard set to represent the action stages for the organisation.

Reduce all readily controlled noise

Before embarking on a complex and expensive programme of

acoustic insulation, etc it is essential to ensure that all easily controlled noise is tackled.

This has been reviewed in Chapter 4, and includes elimination of machine guard rattling, steam leaks, etc.

It is at the end of such an exercise that the need for more sophisticated control measures should be reviewed. The legal requirement to reduce noise is not absolute; it is qualified by reasonable practicability. It is therefore acceptable to take cost and technical complexity into consideration in determining how far noise control measures should be taken.

If the actions taken so far have resulted in low noise levels, say less than 85dB(A) throughout the workplace, then no further action is required other than occasional checks that levels have not increased. However if, as is likely, some noisy activities are left, the remaining steps for hearing protection should be followed.

Establish hearing protection zones
(see NAW, Regulation 9)

A hearing protection exercise which requires employees to wear earmuffs or plugs must be unambiguous. In particular, there must be no doubt about exactly where protective clothing is required. Thus, the boundary of a protection zone must be clearly defined and marked with yellow lines. Notices should make it obvious that hearing protectors are required within the marked area. Remember that the notices should comply with the Safety Signs Regulations 1980 and British Standard 5378. They should illustrate hearing protectors within a blue circle, and have the wording "hearing protection must be worn".

A point covered in Chapter 5 was whether to allow short-term access to the zone, without hearing protectors. In practice, this results in a breakdown of the discipline of using protectors, and should be resisted. It should be made clear to everyone, including senior managers, that protectors must be worn at all times within the zone.

At what noise level should a hearing protection zone be created? In setting the standard, it was suggested that an $L_{EP,d}$ between 85 and 90dB(A) would be set. If the 90dB(A) $L_{EP,d}$ were selected, then noise zones should be created wherever the workplace noise exceeds 90dB(A), assuming that some employees will spend a full 8 hours in the noise zone. If employees spend less than 8 hours in the noise zone, there may be a temptation to increase the dB(A) level at which zones are created, on the grounds that the shorter exposure time will bring down the L_{EP} level. In practice it is probably wiser to zone all areas where the level exceeds 90dB(A) knowing that then no one can possibly experience an L_{EP} higher than this level.

In the event, as was seen in Chapter 3, this question was put on an unambiguous footing by Regulation 9 of the Noise at Work Regulations 1989.

Check the adequacy of hearing protectors
(see NAW, Regulation 8)

It was explained in Chapter 5, that hearing protectors should be selected to suit the environment in which they are used. In other words, the protectors should be particularly efficient at any noise frequencies which are dominant in the workplace, and should reduce the effective dB(A) level by an adequate amount.

This is not to suggest that a major study involving frequency analysis and complicated calculation is required every time hearing protectors are selected. If the noise level is, say, 95dB(A) and clearly does not consist of "pure tone" frequency, then the vast majority of protectors are likely to be suitable and the selection can be made on the basis of comfort and cost.

For higher noise levels however, it is worth selecting the protectors more carefully. This involves subtracting the attenuation figures for the hearing protectors under consideration, from the frequency analysis of workplace noise. This gives the effective frequency breakdown for the protected individual. If this analysis is compared with the A-weighting curve, the effective new dB(A) level can be obtained.

If this exercise seems rather daunting, it may be possible to persuade the suppliers of the protectors to advise on the effectiveness of their models in a particular environment. If you wish to assess a wide range of protectors, it may be of interest to know that a number of computer programs exist which greatly simplify the process. For example, the Steel Castings Research Association has a program which compares the characteristics of a wide range of hearing protectors with a particular noisy environment, and identifies which protectors would be most suitable.

Establish effective enforcement of hearing protector use (see NAW, Regulations 8 and 10)

By far the most common cause of breakdown in a hearing protection programme, is the failure of employees to wear their protective equipment. In the main, this represents a communications problem and must be tackled by publicity and training. However, the fall back position should also be established so that everyone understands the action the company will take when hearing protectors are not worn.

Companies vary in their disciplinary procedures, and there is no reason why the procedure used here should be any different from that used for other breaches of discipline. This is likely to entail informal and formal documented warnings, followed ultimately by removal from the job or dismissal. If the procedures are properly presented, and if it is clear that all management is subjected to the same rules, it is very unlikely that employees and their representatives will oppose such action.

In practice, of course, the involving of a formal disciplinary procedure should be a very rare event. Protective equipment enforcement is primarily a matter of effective management and supervision. Thus the training, job description, etc, of relevant management should include the importance of maintaining health and safety measures.

Ensure employee training is adequate
(see NAW, Regulation 11)

Many employees do not wear the hearing protectors provided for them. Often management attributes this to stubbornness or even stupidity. However, no one would voluntarily suffer avoidable deafness; it is entirely a problem of communication. It is absolutely essential that employees understand the risk of deafness, and that they appreciate the serious social disability from which they could suffer. It is also important that they know that noise-induced deafness is permanent and that a hearing aid will not help.

All of this calls for a good training programme. If the resource or ability does not exist within the company, then there are a number of independent trainers who can present the message most effectively. In addition, some good films are available which can at least supplement a course of training.

Training never ends, and re-training is necessary periodically to keep the message fresh. In general, employees in noise areas should be re-trained at least every two years, though relatively brief refresher sessions should be adequate for most circumstances.

The above comments have referred to training essentially as a motivation tool, to ensure the use of hearing protectors. However, the training should also include the practical requirements of fitting hearing protectors, cleaning and maintaining protectors, using noise control items, etc.

Set noise specification for new equipment
(see NAW Regulation 12)

The best laid plans for noise control and protection can be ruined by the arrival of a new machine. The workplace noise distribution is changed, noise zones must be redefined, and priorities for noise control are affected.

It is therefore necessary to specify the acceptable noise output from new machinery and to recognise that, if the specification is exceeded, there will be significant implications for hearing conservation. Unfortunately, the simple approach of merely defining a maximum dB(A) level for a new machine is no use in practice. This is equivalent to trying to buy a new fire by specifying the temperature it should produce. The dB(A) level is not a characteristic of a machine, and the noise level a new machine will produce depends to a large extent upon the surroundings in which it is placed.

Thus, whilst it is entirely appropriate to make a policy decision that no new machine should be introduced which takes the workplace noise level, say, over 90dB(A), it is not easy to predict whether a particular machine will have that result. It is necessary to ask the machine suppliers to specify what noise level the machine will produce at working positions in your particular workplace. If you wish to undertake the calculation in-house, then you will need to know the "sound power level" from the new machine and consult the acoustic textbooks in the bibliography to convert the power level to a dB(A) level for a specific point in a particular environment.

Review the response to audiogram measurements

There are many benefits in undertaking audiometric tests of employees who work in noisy areas. They can demonstrate the importance which management places upon the problem, and can identify deafness at a sufficiently early stage to take action which prevents serious disablement.

However, it is common to see a company introduce a programme of audiometry without recognising its implications. There is no point in obtaining information about the extent of employees' deafness unless you are going to do something as a result. Therefore, before any audiometric tests are undertaken, you must be able to answer the question "Exactly what will you do when you detect that an employee is partially deaf?"

Clearly, *some* response has to be made. To ignore the information would be irresponsible. An appropriate response could be to explain the findings to the employee, to retrain him or her in the use of hearing protectors, to increase supervision of the use of protectors, and to retest his or her hearing regularly. However, until the systems are in place to ensure that this can be done effectively, audiometry will serve little purpose.

Check policies and procedures

All companies with more than five employees must have a written statement of their safety policy.

This is required to include details of the arrangements for ensuring employees' health and safety. To be effective, the safety policy must be well written, frequently updated, and actively promoted by management. If noise is a particular workplace hazard, it is entirely appropriate to refer to this in the policy, and to state what control and protection measures are to be taken.

There are many other policy and procedure documents which may require revision to include a new approach to noise. For example, conditions of employment may have to refer to the requirement to use hearing protection. There might also be specific systems of work or permits, which should include the requirement for noise control or protection. Personnel and training procedures may be required to monitor the issue and instruction programme for hearing protectors. Finally, purchase procedures and specifications should be prepared so that no one can bring equipment into the workplace without first evaluating its impact on noise levels.

Check internal review mechanism

Once a company's approach to noise is fully resolved, it is necessary to recognise the possibility that future changes in law or medical knowledge might require a change in policy. It might also be that changes become desirable in the light of experience. For example, following employees' reaction to a particular hearing protector.

It is therefore worth asking whether the company has a suitable mechanism for periodically reviewing the noise situation, and making changes where appropriate. A likely vehicle is a high-level committee, for example a company or group safety committee, which has overall policy making authority in this field. If noise is made a fixed item on their agenda for, say, an annual review, then actions on noise can be consistent and co-ordinated throughout the company, and the response to noise can be kept up to date.

Check documentation

Finally, having made an impeccable response to the problems of noise, put it in writing.

Records of noise surveys, issue of hearing protection, employee training, audiogram measurements, etc are essential. They are the basis from which the next level of actions will be taken. It must also be recognised that noise-induced deafness is an active area for legal proceedings, and documentation of actions may be required as evidence.

Good record keeping requires advance planning. Records which might seem adequate now, can be quite incomprehensible when retrieved in 10 years' time. The records need to be unambiguous, authoritative, and stored so that they can be readily retrieved. Consider your existing records and ask whether you can demonstrate what noise levels existed throughout the plant in 1980. Can you also show what hearing protectors a particular individual had been issued with, when they were last inspected, and when he or she was trained in their use? If answering these questions presents any problems, then the record keeping system would probably benefit from an overhaul.

Nomogram for calculation of LEP

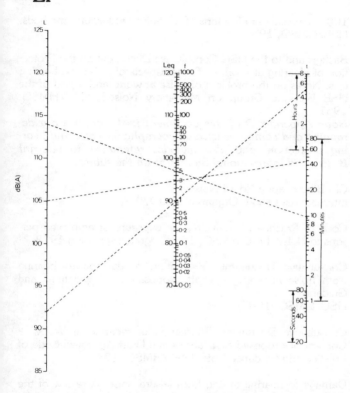

(1) For each exposure connect sound level dB(A) with exposure duration t. and read fractional exposure f. on centre scale.

(2) Add together values of f. received during one day to obtain total value of f.

(3) Read equivalent continuous sound level Leq. opposite total value of f.

Reproduced by permission of the Controller of Her Majesty's Stationery Office. (NB: Leq abbreviation now replaced by LEP.)

Bibliography

100 practical applications for noise reduction methods. HSE/HMSO, 1983

Background to the HSC Consultative Document on the Protection of Hearing at Work – "Some aspects of noise and hearing loss: Notes on the problem of noise at work, and report of the HSE Working Group on Machinery Noise". HSC/HMSO, 1981
Note: Appendix D of this document itself contains a wide-ranging and comprehensive bibliography on noise and hearing protection, and also includes references to relevant British and International Standards on the subject.

CIS Bibliography No 14 Noise.
International Labour Organisation, 1979

Code of Practice for reducing the exposure of employed persons to Noise. HSE/HMSO, 1972, eighth impression 1978

Consultative Document "Prevention of damage to hearing from noise at work" – Draft proposals for Regulations and Guidance.
HSC/HMSO, 1987

Consultative Document "Protection of Hearing at Work" – Content of proposed Regulations and Draft Approved Code of Practice and Guidance Note. HSC/HMSO, 1981

Damage to hearing arising from leisure noise: A review of the literature.
HMSO 1985

Audiometry in industry – Discussion Document.
HMSO, 1978

HSE Noise Guide No 1: Legal duties of employers to prevent damage to hearing

HSE Noise Guide No 2: Legal duties of designers, manufacturers, importers and suppliers to prevent damage to hearing.

The above two guides are available together in one booklet HMSO (ISBN 0 11 885512 3)

HSE Noise Guide No 3: Equipment and procedures for noise surveys

HSE Noise 4: Engineering control of noise

HSE Noise Guide No 5: Types and selection of personal ear protectors

HSE Noise Guide No 6: Training for competent persons

HSE Noise Guide No 7: Procedures for noise testing

HSE Noise Guide No 8: Exemption from certain Noise at Work requirements
HSE Noise Guides 3-8 are available from HMSO.

Occupational Deafness – Report by the Industrial Injuries Advisory Council. Cmnd 8749.
HMSO, 1982

A small-scale survey into the use of audiometry in practice.
Rupert Taylor. HSE, 1988
(HSE Contract Research Report No.3 (1988))

Noise at Work.
Action by HSE's field forces and agencies 1984-86.
HSE, 1988

Sharland I, Woods Practical Guide to Noise Control. Woods of Colchester, 1972

Taylor R Noise. Pelican, 1979 (third edition)

Webb J D (Editor) Noise Control in Industry, Sound Research Laboratories Limited, 1976 (second edition 1978)

Appendix 1: Audiometry in practice

In 1988 the Health and Safety Executive published the results of a small-scale survey which had looked at some of the audiometry programmes operated voluntarily by organisations in this country.

The aims of the survey were to establish whether those organisations carrying out audiometry actually set objectives and monitored them, and what use was made of the audiometric results in practice.

This appendix gives a brief summary of some of the principal findings of the survey.

The survey, based on interviews, covered 12 employers, ranging from nationalised industries and multinational companies to small manufacturing firms.

The interview was built round five questions:
(a) Why do you test?
(b) Who do you test?
(c) When do you test?
(d) What do you do with the results?
(e) How do you test?

The final question was asked in a restricted form only so as not to distract from the main purpose of the questions by concentrating on the technical quality of the audiometric testing itself.

Audiometry is carried out for two reasons:
(a) to protect the employer
(b) because audiometry is a "good thing".

The absence of formal policies for action triggered by predetermined hearing levels or changes in hearing levels is attributable to the general belief that hearing protection is a complete answer to the noise problem.

Adverse trends in hearing levels, when discovered, are taken to mean that ear protection is not being correctly applied. Renewed effort to improve the use of hearing protection follows by means of persuasion of those concerned. The audiometric test results are used as "ammunition in the battle to gain better observance of hearing conservation measures".

In all cases it was found that the carrying out of audiometry was accompanied by education about noise hazards.

The conclusions to be drawn from the answers given to the survey questions are:

(a) that among employers who practice audiometry, hearing levels are not deteriorating to a significant extent because of the use of hearing protection;
(b) that if hearing thresholds rise significantly they will be detected by audiometry;
(c) that audiometry is an educational tool which brings about more assiduous use of hearing protection;
(d) that hearing protection and audiometry taken together are believed to make organisations "noise safe".

HSE Contract Research Report No. 3/1988 – *A small-scale survey into the use of audiometry in practice* Rupert Taylor, Consultant.

Appendix 2: Noise at work – action by HSE's field forces and agencies 1984-86

This 1988 report gives an account of the concentrated efforts by HSE's inspectorates (Factories, Mines, Quarries and Agricultural) and agencies (Petroleum Engineering Division and Railways) to achieve a better measure of compliance with the noise control standards current before the present Noise at Work Regulations 1989 (NAW) took effect on 1.1.90.

The 1972 "Code of Practice for reducing the exposure of employed persons to noise" set limits of noise exposure and recommended a range of measures for noise control.

The HSE initiative, prior to the final stages of consultation before NAW came into operation, set about the following:

(a) asking employers to take a fresh look at their noise problems;
(b) assessing the effectiveness of engineering controls and the provision of hearing protection where noise could not be adequately controlled by engineering means;
(c) giving impetus to, and where necessary enforcing, further efforts by employers to reduce their employees' noise exposure, and
(d) attempting to gauge the effectiveness of the initiatives themselves.

A brief summary of some of the main findings follows.

Compliance with the 1972 code of Practice

Factory inspectorate

	Yes	No
Noise hazard areas identified	42%	58%
Employees aware of noise hazard area	57%	43%
Engineering controls reasonably practicable	53%	47%
Some engineering controls provided	15%	85%
Suitable hearing protection provided	71%	29%
Adequate training, instruction and supervision in the use of hearing protection	28%	72%

(a) In firms making hearing protection available, 63% of them did not back its use by instruction and training.

(b) On average only 40% of those exposed to noise were seen to be wearing protection.

(c) In half of the companies reported on only 25% or less of those exposed to noise were using protection.

(d) Enforcement action is valuable because after enforcement officers' visits 75% of the employers concerned made some improvements.

(e) After the general survey the Factory Inspectorate decided to develop initiatives through special projects and National Interest Groups.

Mines and Quarries Inspectorate

(a) The initiative in mines and quarries was to concentrate on the identification of noise sources. Whilst enclosure techniques have only limited application to quarries, sound-proofed control cabins have proved suitable and have also aided airborne dust control. Noise reductions of nearly 30 dB(A) have been reported.

(b) Examples of success in specific fields at coal mines are reported covering such things as silencing of locomotives, free-steered vehicles and loading machines; the use of silencers with auxiliary fans; and the relocation of working positions so that they are outside any identified 90 dB(A) noise zones.

Agricultural Inspectorate

(a) The major success story in agriculture is in relation to tractors. Reductions from levels in excess of 100 dB(A) to less than 80 dB(A) have been achieved in just over a decade.

(b) A major difficulty lies in the problem of establishing operator exposure periods.

(c) The industry's own awareness of noise problems has been significantly raised over recent years.

Petroleum Engineering Division (Department of Energy)

(a) No offshore installation may operate without a valid certificated of fitness. Noise is extensively considered before certificates are issued so appropriate steps are taken to reduce noise at the design and construction stages.

(b) Areas where noise levels are in excess of 88 dB(A), where during certain operations a lower noise level is not possible, are designated "restricted".
Certifying authorities are keeping noise levels offshore under review.

Railway Inspectorate

(a) The most difficult and far reaching work has been the Inspectorate's attempt to reduce the noise level in locomotive cabs, but a programme of research and development is in hand to reduce noise levels in existing locomotives to 85 dB(A) and in new locomotives to 82 dB(A).

(b) Other areas of difficulty include high levels of noise when running engines under test; warning sounds' audibility when hearing protection is being worn, and the use of ear plugs by workers with dirty hands.

Conclusion

The conclusion of the HSE report is that awareness levels of the problems of noise have been enhanced and that the enforcement and advisory initiatives prior to NAW have gone some way towards conditioning people to accept the statutory standards which NAW laid down in conformity with the 1986 EC directive.

Noise at Work – Action by HSE's field forces and agencies 1984-86 Health and Safety Executive.

Appendix 3: Damage to Hearing Arising from Leisure Noise – A review of the Literature [1985]

The Health and Safety Executive commissioned the Medical Research Council (MRC) Institute of Hearing Research to produce a critical review of the relevant existing literature covering all noisy leisure activities, including some for which the Health and Safety Commission and the Health and Safety Executive have no legislative responsibility.

The purpose of publishing the report was to promote informed discussion and to stimulate further research where it appears information remains inadequate.

The reason for commissioning the study was the concern, parallel with that about the growing risk of adverse ill-effects from industrial noise, about the possible consequences of exposure to high noise levels in leisure activities such as discotheques.

Three aspects of the problem of leisure noise are of particular relevance to the HSC's and HSE's responsibilities under the Health and Safety at Work, etc Act 1974:

(a) Risk of hearing damage to those whose profession or occupation involves them in high sound level environments (eg disc jockeys, musicians).

(b) Risk to those who are not themselves at work, but who might be subject to risk from attending professionally organised noisy leisure activities.

(c) The possibility that noise exposure in leisure activities will contribute significantly to damage sustained by those working or starting to work in noisy industries.

Conclusions

The extensive literature on possible auditory hazard from non-occupational noise exposure was reviewed and found to be disappointing in its poor design, methodology and reporting. However, certain conclusions were possible:

(a) The major source of auditory hazard, in population terms, from non-workplace noise is amplified music. Precise conclusions about it cannot be drawn because the literature gives widely different estimates.

The Noise Immission Levels (NIL) differ by about 5dB and the numbers exposed by a factor of three to seven.

"On the very highest estimates, the hazard from non-occupational noise would vie as a societal source of impairment and disability with occupational noise of 85-90dB(A) (Leq equivalent to eight hours daily exposure). On the lowest estimates for both NIL and numbers affected, the equivalent occupational noise would be about 80dB(A)."

(b) For the individual, the worst-cases of discothèque and personal cassette player exposure represent real risks. Shooting of firearms without proper hearing protection is also pinpointed but because levels and exposures are under voluntary control it is difficult to estimate risk.

(c) For the population, the numbers receiving worst-case exposures are not known accurately.

Non-occupational noise is only likely to be a material part of the overall noise exposure experienced by workers where their noise exposure at work is substantially less than 90dB(A) (leq equivalent to 8 hours daily exposure).

The numbers significantly exposed to non-occupational noise would certainly be a factor complicating statutory provision for hearing conservation if occupational exposure limits were set at 80dB(A).

An outstanding need is for a large random sample whole-population survey of exposure rates and patterns for leisure noise in general and amplified music in particular.

Damage to Hearing arising from Leisure noise: A Review of the Literature HMSO.

Index